EDITORIAL RESEARCH REPORTS ON

The American Future

Timely Reports to Keep
Journalists, Scholars and the Public
Abreast of Developing Issues, Events and Trends

Published by Congre
1414 22nd S
Washington,

D1456344

About the Cover

The cover was designed by staff artist Richard Pottern. Art Director Howard Chapman.

PRINTED IN THE UNITED STATES OF AMERICA, FEBRUARY 1976

Editor, Hoyt Gimlin
Editorial Assistant, Diane Huffman
Production Manager, I. D. Fuller

Library of Congress Cataloging in Publication Data

Congressional Quarterly, Inc.
  The American future.

  Includes bibliographies and index.
  1. Forecasting. 2. United States—Social conditions—1960- I. Title.
  HN65.C613 1976   309.1'73'0925   76-2658
  ISBN 0-87187-086-X

Contents

Foreword

An urge amounting to a compulsion has seized upon Americans in this bicentennial year to gaze reflectively and a bit wistfully at the past. It's entirely appropriate after 200 years of nationhood for a people to pause and take stock of their country and the human condition that prevails therein. But there are social philosophers who suggest the current nostalgia binge is rooted in something deeper and murkier. There seems to be a popular yearning, expressed in a thousand ways, to retreat to or rediscover some yesteryear in which "things were better."

This kind of preoccupation with the past may be a symptom of a national malaise—or it may be merely a passing fad. Regardless, there is ample cause to say, as John Hamer does in this book's opening report, "America's Next Century," that many people prefer to look backward with nostalgia than forward to the future. The future, they fear, doesn't look as good as it used to. That perception may or may not turn out to be faulty, but it does seem to reflect the dominant national mood at this moment in history. This mood has been colored no doubt by the recent national traumas of Vietnam, Watergate and economic faltering. In the words of F. David Mathews when he was sworn in as Secretary of Health, Education and Welfare, this is "the age when things did not work out as we thought they would."

Has the traditional American buoyancy and optimism been permanently dulled by today's realities and modest expectations? The multiplying number of "futurologists" who dot the academic landscape and think-tank centers are no more of one mind on this question than they are on any other. And Editorial Research Reports is not in the soothsaying business. What this book attempts is not to provide the answers—only with divine guidance or an overabundance of audacity would we try. It seeks instead to shed light on the questions that are being asked in a number of areas important to the nation's future.

The report titles listed on another page indicate the breadth of this undertaking. These are only some of the questions facing this country. But they are enough, we hope, to give the reader perspective on the American future.

Hoyt Gimlin
Editor

February 1976
Washington, D.C.

AMERICA'S NEXT CENTURY

by

John Hamer

Jan. 9
1976

AMERICA'S **NEXT** **CENTURY**

1976 **2076**

W HEN THE UNITED STATES began its centennial year in 1876, the national spirit was high. Americans were justly proud of their past and confident about their future. It was a time to look forward, with hope and anticipation. The Philadelphia Centennial Exhibition later that year was an exciting smorgasbord of the technological marvels that would revolutionize American life in the years to come. "America's independence had survived its first century, the nation's great progress was obvious, and the future seemed assured," wrote historian William Peirce Randel in describing the 1876 New Year celebrations. "It was a time to make merry as never before."[1]

In contrast, America begins its bicentennial year in 1976 with a nagging sense of doubt about the past and uncertainty about the future. Many Americans are deeply concerned over the national condition today and sincerely worried about the years ahead. Some are unhappy with what America has come to represent among its own people and in the eyes of the world; many would rather look backward with nostalgia than forward with anticipation. Still, they wonder what America's next century will bring for the individual citizen, what it will mean for the state of the nation, and how it will change this country's role in the world. There is a widespread feeling that America is at a kind of turning point, facing some hard choices in the near future which will demand harsh departures from past and present policies. The American dream has changed, to say the least.

Some of the reasons why Americans feel this way are evident. The nation is still suffering from the effects of simultaneous inflation and recession which have violated all the rules of the economists. It has not yet come to grips with the full meaning of the long, divisive Vietnam War—the first clear loss in the nation's history. The Watergate scandal led to the first presidential resignation in U.S. history, and now Americans are being reminded that similar abuses of governmental power occurred under a succession of previous presidents. The nation's foreign and domestic intelligence services are being exposed to un-

---

[1] *Centennial—American Life in 1876* (1969), p. 1.

3

Hazards of Forecasting

The hazards of predicting the future are vividly demonstrated by recalling a few famous forecasts of the past. It is unlikely that any major enterprise was ever undertaken without some expert predicting that it would fail. A panel of Spanish sages in 1490 examined Columbus' plan for his voyage and came up with six reasons why it was impossible. In 1784 the Marquis de Condorcet, a leading French philosopher, wrote: "The great probability is that we will have fewer great changes and fewer large revolutions to expect from the future than from the past."

The errant predictions seemed to increase with advances in science and technology. Many experts insisted that a new invention called the railroad would kill its passengers, who would not be able to breathe when traveling at such high speeds. A week before the Wright brothers' flight at Kitty Hawk, *The New York Times* editorially advised another airplane inventor to turn to "more useful employment." In 1940, *Scientific American* wrote that a rocket bomb was "too farfetched to be considered,"

Among the best prophets have been science-fiction writers, whose imaginations predicted many scientific developments. Jules Verne foresaw both submarines and voyages to the moon. Just as prophetic was Hugo Gernsback, one of the first American science-fiction writers, who correctly predicted radar, television, communications satellites and night baseball.

precedented public scrutiny, and their record of involvement in assassinations, character defamations and invasions of privacy has shocked many persons. In the words of F. David Mathews when he was sworn in as Secretary of Health, Education, and Welfare, this is "the age when things did not work out as we thought they would."

In addition, the nation has had a taste of energy shortages, although the goal of energy independence is still remote. Most citizens remain unwilling to follow the strict conservation measures necessary to attain that goal. Meanwhile, the drive to clean up the environment and stop pollution is no longer the national crusade it was in the early 1970s. Urban areas keep sprawling over the surrounding countryside, while central cities continue to deteriorate physically and fiscally. Crime is a national epidemic, and few anti-crime measures seem to work.

Internationally, the United States is facing strident criticism from Third World nations which resent its prosperity and power, while it treads a tricky path of détente and alliance with the Soviet Union, China, Western Europe and Japan. The terrible threat of nuclear war still hangs over the world, with the increasing likelihood that small countries or terrorist groups soon will acquire nuclear armaments—an ominous prospect when calls for redistribution of world income are heard ever more frequently. Raymond Vernon, director of Harvard University's Center for International Affairs, has said: "There is abroad in the world today a sense of the end of something and the beginning of something new."[2]

The 20th century clearly has been "the American century," but at great cost to the world's energy, food and other natural resources. Americans waste an appalling amount of what they use. If all of the world's people were raised to the American living standard today, current resource supplies would be exhausted. Even at present rates of world resource use and population growth, some analysts believe that a crunch will come during the next century. The authors of *The Limits to Growth* (1972), a report to the Club of Rome's "Project on the Predicament of Mankind," declared: "If present growth trends in world population, industrialization, pollution, food production and resource depletion continue unchanged, the limits to growth on this planet will be reached sometime within the next one hundred years."[3] Although many debunked this computer-based study because it did not account for potential advances in science and technology, subsequent studies have reached similar conclusions.[4]

Proliferation of Futures Research Organizations

Rising concern about the future has been accompanied—and to some extent caused—by the proliferation of groups that make the study of the future a full-time effort. The words "futurism" and "futurology" have found a place in modern dictionaries, and many "futurists" or "future research specialists" have been practicing their skills for several years. Forecasting and predictions are nothing new, of course. Prophets, mystics, astrologers, psychics and other assorted soothsayers have been around throughout history. What is new is the attempt to make forecasting less of an art and more of a science.

Modern futurism dates from the founding of the Rand Corporation after World War II. Its initial studies dealt primarily with military and space predictions.[5] Rand soon was joined by the Hudson Institute and Stanford Research Institute, among others, which generally concentrated on strategic, scientific and technological issues. The Center for the Study of Democratic In-

---

[2] Quoted by Robert Pittman, *St. Petersburg* (Fla.) *Times*, June 30, 1975.

[3] Donella H. Meadows, Dennis L. Meadows, Jorgen Randers, William W. Behrens III, *The Limits to Growth* (1972), p. 23.

[4] See, for instance, Mihajlo Mesarovic and Eduard Pestel, *Mankind at the Turning Point* (1974), p. vii.

[5] See "Directions of Policy Research," *E.R.R.*, 1975 Vol. II, pp. 725-744.

stitutions, founded in 1959, was one of the first organizations to undertake social, economic and other non-military research and forecasting.

These so-called "think tanks" have been joined recently by a succession of groups dedicated to studying a broad range of "alternative futures." Citizens, government agencies, universities and industries have formed countless centers and institutes to probe the future. A 1973 study by The Futures Group, one of these new organizations, found that almost 900 separate groups had completed at least one future-oriented study or project within the last few years. "Futures literature" has been recognized as a separate category in many libraries and bookstores, and thousands of items have been listed in bibliographies on the subject. Courses in futurology have been offered by hundreds of colleges and universities.

A good indication of rising interest in futurism was the second general assembly of the World Future Society, held in Washington, D.C., in June 1975. It attracted 2,500 people, more than twice as many as expected.[6] It was attended by representatives of the Commission on the Year 2000, sponsored by the American Academy of Arts and Sciences, and the Institute for the Future, formed by a consortium of companies including Monsanto, Du Pont and Chase Manhattan Bank. There were members of numerous academic groups, such as the Princeton Center for Alternative Futures, Studies of the Future at the University of Houston, and the System Dynamics Group of Massachusetts Institute of Technology. Among the participants were Herman Kahn of the Hudson Institute, Alvin Toffler, author of *Future Shock* (1970), and Daniel Bell of Harvard University, author of *The Coming of Post-Industrial Society* (1973).

The federal government also has become involved in the futures game. The Office of Technology Assessment (OTA) was set up in 1972 to help Congress evaluate the potential future impact of technology for the purposes of legislation.[7] When the Congressional Budget Office was created in 1974, its staff was directed to assess the long-term budgetary impacts of new legislation; amendments to the same act required the federal budget, starting in fiscal year 1977, to include five-year revenue and expenditure projections. A House of Representatives resolution requires all committees to develop future research and forecasting capabilities, and a new futures division was set up in the Congressional Research Service at the Library of Congress.

---

[6] The society, founded in 1966 as a non-profit organization to encourage the study of alternative futures, publishes a magazine called *The Futurist*, "a journal of forecasts, trends and ideas about the future."

[7] See *Congressional Quarterly 1972 Almanac*, pp. 692-693.

Future Research Methods

Several methods for probing the future have emerged in recent years. Some critics have dismissed them as mere rituals, but futurists say they are useful. They include:

Delphi Polls—Developed at the Rand Corporation as a way to incorporate experts' judgments into forecasting. Questionnaires are distributed asking participants to predict when certain technological or social developments might occur. Results are collected, tabulated and returned, so participants may reconsider their judgments. A third or fourth round repeats the process until a consensus is reached or a marked polarization develops.

World Game—Developed by Buckminster Fuller, this is an unstructured, free-form method generally involving a large group of people in a workshop exercise. Participants pool available information and resources and "brainstorm" on how to solve world problems such as hunger, housing, disease, pollution and tyranny. They generally follow Fuller's theme of "conscious evolution" for humanity, based on such principles as "more with less."

Syncon—Developed by the Committee for the Future, a nonprofit organization dedicated to bringing future options into the public arena for decision and action. Participants are mostly average citizens from a wide range of disciplines and backgrounds. They are divided into groups. with each unit assigned a problem such as energy, nuclear weapons or population, and asked to solve it "to everyone's satisfaction."

Club of Rome—The primary technique used in reports to the Club of Rome is the computer simulation method originated by Dr. Jay W. Forrester of the System Dynamics Group at the Massachusetts Institute of Technology. In *Urban Dynamics* (1969) and *World Dynamics* (1971), Forrester developed the method of extrapolating present trends into the next century by programing a computer to show what could happen.

In the executive branch, the Defense Department and other national security groups long have been in the forecasting business, along with such agencies as the Census Bureau, the Bureau of Labor Statistics and the Agriculture Department. But recently other agencies such as the Federal Aviation Administration and the National Science Foundation have begun making long-range projections for policy-making purposes. An Ad Hoc Interagency Futures Group was formed a few years ago to stimulate discussion among government officials. It has conducted a detailed study of alternative federal budgets for the year 2000 and is doing a survey on "the future of governance."[8] The National Environmental Policy Act, which took effect in 1970, has advanced futuristic thinking by requiring federal agencies to consider the environmental impact of proposed actions.[9]

---

[8] Constance Holden, "Futurism: Gaining a Toehold in Public Policy," *Science*, July 11, 1975, p. 122.
[9] See "Environmental Policy," *E.R.R.*, 1974 Vol. II, pp. 945-964.

More than 20 states and cities have citizens' organizations involved in future research and planning. They include California Tomorrow, Seattle 2000, Goals for Dallas, Hawaii 2000, Alternatives for Washington, Iowa 2000, Massachusetts Tomorrow, Atlanta 2000, Goals for Georgia, and the Commission on Minnesota's Future. In addition, about 100 of the nation's largest corporations now employ "house futurists" to explore future alternatives and keep companies abreast of emerging trends in business and industry.

Can all these ardent future research groups have any real value in assessing America's future? Estimates of their potential effectiveness vary. Futurists often say that what they come up with are the right questions rather than the right answers. Robert Lamson of the National Science Foundation has criticized what he calls the lack of quality control in the field, which gives rise to a lot of "sloppy thinking being expressed in sloppy language."[10] Robert Jungk of the Center for Future Research in West Berlin, one of a number of European futurist organizations, has faulted some groups for merely reinforcing widely held judgments. "If someone comes up with a radically different diagnosis, it is discarded.... Present future research simply lacks social imagination."[11] Other futurists defend the field as useful if inexact. Futurists reject the saying that if one takes care of the present, the future will take care of itself.

Outlook for Individual Americans

A S MUCH AS Americans are concerned about the nation's future, most are primarily concerned about what tomorrow may bring for them, their children and their grandchildren. It is difficult for most people to look beyond that, and they are less inclined to worry about their remote descendants. But history has shown that people are willing to make great sacrifices in the short term. Indeed, probably the most important factor in the complex equation of the country's future is the way individuals will respond to crises ahead.

[10] Quoted by Constance Holden in *Science*, July 11, 1975, p. 124.
[11] Vic Cox, "Futurist Robert Jungk: The Optimistic Pessimist," *Human Behavior*, November 1974, p. 29.

Undeniably, many of the experts are pessimistic about what individual Americans will face in the future. At the World Future Society's meeting, bleak predictions abounded. Sociologist Daniel Bell of Harvard University described "the end of American exceptionalism" and Alvin Toffler called the energy and economic problems evidence of "the general crisis of industrial society." Jib Fowles of the University of Houston's Studies of the Future program said that "the community of futurists...holds with near unanimity that what awaits man will be upsetting."[12]

Economist Kenneth Boulding said that the most significant change in American attitudes in recent years is the drift from individual responsibility to societal responsibility. Our grandparents instinctively blamed themselves if things went wrong, Boulding said, but we blame others. Guaranteed jobs regardless of performance, government bailouts of corporations, and attribution of crime to society rather than criminals are examples of this trend. A recent study by the Institute of Life Insurance in Washington, D.C., found that many Americans are abandoning the traditional work ethic and adopting a "no risk" attitude feeling that they should be guaranteed housing, income, education and health.[13]

Much has been made of the idea that the United States, along with most of the western world, is moving toward what Daniel Bell described, in his 1973 book, as the "post-industrial society." Bell, along with political scientist Zbigniew Brzezinski, futurist Herman Kahn and election analyst Kevin P. Phillips, argues that a post-industrial society is one in which knowledge and technology replace manufacturing and physical labor as the dominant facts of economic and social life.[14] "Since World War II," Phillips wrote in *Mediacracy* (1975), "the United States has been in the vanguard of a new, post-industrial economic era increasingly built around the sale of services and knowledge rather than manufactured products." The post-industrial class is seen as less interested in material acquisition and consumption than in reading and recreational activity.

Possible Alterations in Lifestyle of Citizens

Will Americans be given the luxury of more leisure time in the future? Many have predicted that a four-day work week is coming, but it seems as remote as ever to most working people. Some companies have experimented with flexible working hours and other means of providing workers more job satisfaction, but 9-

---

[12] Quoted in Conservation Foundation *Letter*, June 1975, p. 1.

[13] "A Culture in Transformation: Toward a Different Societal Ethic?" Institute of Life Insurance, Trend Analysis Program, Trend Report No. 12, Dec. 3, 1975, press release.

[14] See Warden Moxley, "Post-Industrial Politics: A Guide to 1976," *Congressional Quarterly Weekly Report*, Nov. 15, 1975, pp. 2475-2478.

to-5 is still routine for most Americans. One widely heard prediction is that high-speed communications technology will eliminate the need for many workers to come to the office at all. Some believe that workers soon will start "tele-commuting" from neighborhood—and later home—telecommunications centers equipped with two-way cable TV channels. "When production is properly automated even in service industries," wrote Norman Macrae, deputy editor of the British magazine *The Economist*, in a recent special report on America's future, "probably 60 per cent of American breadwinners will be brainworkers. A brainworker can much more easily dispatch his work than himself to the office."[15]

Along with the telecommunications revolution, Macrae believes, will come a return by Americans to small towns and rural areas, away from the big cities and sprawling suburbs. This trend has already begun. In the words of demographer Calvin L. Beale: "The vast rural-to-urban migration of people that was the common pattern of U.S. population movement in the decades after World War II has been halted and, on balance, even reversed."[16] Non-metropolitan areas are growing faster than metropolitan areas for the first time in this century, and the rural migration shows no signs of abating.

With the advances in communication and transportation that are sure to come in the future, many more areas than at present may be considered desirable dwelling places. The next century is likely to produce almost service-free automobiles made largely of plastic, automated urban mass transit systems and noiseless railroads, according to a recent forecast by McGraw-Hill Publishing Company's economics department. Improvements in transportation, however, may be accompanied by restrictions on mobility. Numerous cities and states are already trying to control their growth rates, and some analysts foresee tight regulations over the freedom to move. Such drastic measures as city quotas, residency permits, migrant fees and population controls are envisioned.[17]

Another American institution widely expected to undergo further change is the family. Already, a much wider variety of living options are acceptable than just a few years ago, when the patriarchal family was almost mandatory. Feminist Gloria Steinem has said: "There must be a variety of options—so that it becomes an honorable solution to remain single, to live with a group of people, to live with another person, to have children or not to have children, and so on."[18] With the widespread accep-

---

[15] "America's Third Century: A Survey," *The Economist*, Oct. 25, 1975, p. 39.
[16] See "Rural Migration," *E.R.R.*, 1975 Vol. II, pp. 581-600.
[17] See "Restrictions on Urban Growth," *E.R.R.*, 1973 Vol. I, pp. 85-104.
[18] Quoted in "What Kind of Future for America," *U.S. News & World Report*, July 7, 1975, p. 47. See also, "Marriage: Changing Institution," *E.R.R.*, 1971 Vol. II, pp. 761-777.

tance of contraception in this country, sex is increasingly divorced from reproduction, and this trend is likely to continue as medical breakthroughs make it possible for couples to select the exact time of conception and the sex of their offspring.

What this will mean for American moral values is a matter of debate. Some futurists believe the breakdown of traditional standards will accelerate, while others think a backlash is likely to develop. "There will be more acceptance of the pleasure ethic," said Herman Kahn of the Hudson Institute in a copyrighted interview in *U.S. News & World Report* in 1973, "but the average American will not believe that hedonism is the name of the game—that life's only purpose is happiness."

Continuing Problems of Morals, Medicine, Health

However, advances in medical technology may soon give people access to other sources of pleasure. Already scientists can plant electrodes in animals' brains and by electrical stimulation induce intense pleasure. Rats which have been taught to switch on the electricity at will are said to greatly prefer this experience to food or to their own mates. There is little doubt that the same is possible with human beings. Another potential use of implanted electrodes is to control criminals or other aggressive individuals. This controversial technique clearly would arouse a great debate about civil liberties, but it has been widely predicted.[19]

Some form of national health insurance seems increasingly likely. Diagnostic health-screening devices, undoubtedly linked to computers, will examine patients and produce vital information in minutes. Dramatic advances are predicted in "spare parts" surgery—more organ and limb transplants and use of artificial devices to repair bodily damage or correct defects. Cures for cancer and heart disease—the nation's top killers—are widely expected within the next century. Many medical authorities expect the average life span of Americans, which has doubled in the past 200 years to 70 years today, to increase further. Dr. Charles A. Berry, head of the University of Texas Health Science Center at Houston, says: "I think many Americans will live well into the hundreds" in the next century.[20] Another potential threat, however, is the outbreak of an entirely new disease. "A real plague, incurable and swift, is only a matter of time, according to some public health authorities," wrote Theodore Sturgeon in *Human Behavior* magazine.[21] Whatever else the future may bring, it holds many unknowns.

---

[19] See "Medical Ethics," *E.R.R.*, 1972 Vol. I, pp. 459-478, and "Human Engineering," *E.R.R.*, 1971 Vol. I, pp. 367-386.

[20] Quoted in "What Kind of Future for America," *U.S. News & World Report*, July 7, 1975, p. 47.

[21] "Facing Up to Disaster," *Human Behavior*, November 1974, p. 66.

Prospective State of the Nation

THE HEALTH AND HAPPINESS of individual Americans are keys to the condition and contentment of the nation as a whole. How is the state of the nation likely to change in the next century? The most important factors, many futurists agree, are the extent to which U.S. natural resource and energy supplies prove adequate and how this affects the national economy. These factors, in turn, may determine whether the traditional American system of government can survive. Opinion is deeply divided over the adequacy of future resource and energy supplies. Only two years ago, Americans were being confronted with shortages of vital items and materials on all sides.[22] Many commentators predicted a future of recurrent shortages and decreasing abundance. "We are going to be continuously confronted with choices between higher prices and shortages," predicted Herbert Stein of the Council of Economic Advisers.[23]

Today, some futurists believe that U.S. energy and resource supplies will be adequate to serve the more than 300 million Americans who are expected to inhabit the nation by around the year 2020. Perhaps the most optimistic is Herman Kahn of the Hudson Institute:

> [A]re we running out of energy? The answer is absolutely not. No way. Are we running out of resources? Absolutely not. No way. Are we running out of ability to feed people from a technological and economic point of view? Absolutely not. No way. Can we retain clean air and clean water and esthetic landscape? Absolutely.[24]

It has been said that each American, through the use of energy and technology, has the muscular equivalent of 400 slaves. "We are going to be called upon increasingly to cut back on our standard of living so as to offset population growth in other parts of the world," Benjamin R. Barber, a political science professor at Rutgers University, has predicted. "We're simply going to have to help feed and clothe the poorer nations, because they won't be able to do it on their own, and they have resources that we need."[25]

---

[22] See "Economics of Scarcity," E.R.R., 1973 Vol. II, pp. 821-840.

[23] In a speech Aug. 8, 1973, to the American Bar Association, Washington, D.C.

[24] Quoted by Ned Scharff, The Washington Star, Aug. 3, 1975.

[25] Quoted in "What Kind of Future for America," U.S. News & World Report, July 7, 1975, pp. 45-46.

At the same time, Charles J. Hitch, president of Resources for the Future, Inc., a Washington, D.C., research organization, believes that future resources will be more than adequate if the nation is willing to pay their true social, economic and environmental costs. The world is indeed finite and resources must be husbanded, Hitch believes, through such means as recycling, stockpiling, materials substitution, and conservation, but the supplies are adequate. "I want to say only that none of our studies indicates that doomsday is near," Hitch told a meeting of the American Forestry Association on Oct. 6, 1975. "[T]he resources *are* there, for more than 300 million Americans and for the probable additional billions of the world population."

A number of other analysts also have come around to the belief that resource supplies are probably sufficient for the foreseeable future. Rene Dubos, biologist and environmentalist, has said: "I am not so sure that the main problem is a shortage of resources. I think we have many more resources than we can possibly use. By this I mean that science and technology can certainly discover more resources than we need."[26] Even Dr. Jay W. Forrester, the systems dynamics expert at Massachusetts Institute of Technology, conceded recently that technology may well roll back the physical resource limits predicted in the original report to the Club of Rome three years ago.

On the matter of energy, most experts believe that a virtually unlimited supply will be made available some time within the next century, and some feel that recent energy shortages and price increases are only the last rumblings of the fading fossil fuel era. Nuclear fission and breeder reactors are being pushed by some as the answers to America's energy problems, while others are apprehensive about the accompanying plutonium waste disposal and safety problems.[27]

Critics of conventional nuclear power would expand research and development of nuclear fusion, an essentially unlimited energy source with no harmful byproducts. They also would greatly step up development of solar energy, along with other unconventional sources including wind, geothermal, tidal and ocean thermal-gradient energy, coal gasification and the use of hydrogen as a fuel.[28] However, even if an inexhaustible energy source becomes widely available, many scientists believe there is a limit to how much energy production the global environment can stand. "The limitation will be an ecological limitation," biologist Rene Dubos has said.

[26] Quoted by Paul London in *Business and Society Review*, winter 1974-75, reprinted in *Current*, March 1975, p. 35.

[27] See "Nuclear Safety," *E.R.R.*, 1975 Vol. II, pp. 601-624, and "Nuclear Safeguards," *E.R.R.*, 1974 Vol. II, pp. 865-884.

[28] See "New Energy Sources," *E.R.R.*, 1973 Vol. I, pp. 185-204.

The problem of growth is closely related to resource and energy issues. Since 1972, there have been more than 250 conferences held around the world on growth and its implications. One of the most recent, an international "Limits to Growth" conference held near Houston, Texas, in October 1975, produced a predictable split between futurists who believe that growth is inevitable and desirable and those who feel it is potentially disastrous and must be slowed or controlled.

The polarization in recent years between advocates of "no-growth" and advocates of unlimited growth has lessened somewhat as both sides have conceded that the argument must be defined more precisely in terms of what kind, where, when and how much growth. Even so, many believe that the nation in its next century must abandon the unlimited growth trend of past centuries and move toward a "steady-state" or low-growth society more suitable to the long-term survival of "spaceship earth." One of the chief proponents of this view is economist Herman Daly, editor of the book *Toward a Steady-State Economy* (1973). He argues that constant stocks of population and physical wealth should be maintained at a chosen level. To implement such drastic measures, the nation clearly would need a stronger, more centralized federal government. Some futurists think that such a government is almost inevitable.

Likely Challenges to Traditional American System

Whether the American system of government will be strong enough to survive the challenges of the future without basic structural changes is an open question. There is a widespread feeling among Americans today that the old political institutions, especially Congress, do not work very well. For one thing, there is stubborn resistance to change among politicians and bureaucrats. For another, the facts, issues and problems of today's world often seem too complex to handle effectively under the present system. Respect for governmental authority clearly is dropping. A 1975 Louis Harris survey indicated that, since 1966, public confidence in Congress has fallen from 42 per cent to 14 per cent; confidence in the White House from 41 per cent to 14 per cent; and in the Supreme Court from 51 per cent to 28 per cent. "The gulf between the American public and its leadership has rarely been so wide or deep," Harris said.

But there is a paradox in the American attitude toward government. At the same time, Americans are placing greater demands on the political system and on political leaders than ever before. "We have assigned a new and larger role to the political system," former Special [Watergate] Prosecutor Archibald Cox told the Associated Harvard Alumni on June 12, 1975. "Government has become the forum in which men and

women, business corporations and other organized groups contend for their own interests with all the selfishness and am-
bition, and sometimes the ruthlessness and deceit, that once
characterized the market." And the increasing demand on
government is unlikely to lessen in the foreseeable future.
Several years ago, in the first report of the Commission on the
Year 2000, Chairman Daniel Bell wrote: "The only prediction
about the future that one can make with certainty is that public
authorities will face more problems than they have at any
previous time in history."[29]

Other analysts have expressed similar sentiments. Peter
Schrag wrote recently in *Harper's:*

"The problem now is to restore some semblance of legitimacy and
authority under a wholly new and more limited set of conditions,
conditions where tomorrow may not be better than today, not
much anyway, where the future is gray and flat, where tragedy,
morality and social inequities can't be evaded, and where it's increasingly hard to get a mortgage on tomorrow. No American
politician has ever been able to talk about these things; indeed,
there is no political language in America—not yet—in which they
can be discussed, no language not founded on premises of growth
and expansion, and the country desperately needs such a
language."[30]

However, there is doubt in some minds that any American
politician will be able to fill such a role. And there is hesitancy to
push too hard for action for fear that government will only make
things worse. "My impression today is that most Americans are
distrustful of politicians and politics, that they are irritated by
the government's presence where they think it isn't needed and
irritated by its absence where they think it is needed," Charles
Frankel observed in *Commentary*.[31] Along the same line, Jay
Martin wrote in *Antioch Review:* "It would be utterly false to
conclude...that Americans yearn secretly for strong leaders and
authoritarian rule.... What they most yearn for is no government
and no leaders."[32] If the 1976 presidential campaign is any guide,
Americans may indeed be longing for less government, because
candidate after candidate has come out against the evils of "big
government."

A possible alternative is more local control, as decentralization is seen as the best way to restore people's faith in
government. Karl Hess of the Institute for Policy Studies is
among many advocates of returning governmental power to the

---

[29] "Toward the Year 2000," *Daedalus* (journal of the American Academy of Arts and
Sciences), summer 1967, p. 645.

[30] "America Needs an Establishment," *Harper's*, December 1975, p. 58.

[31] "America Now: A Failure of Nerves?" *Commentary*, July 1975, p. 36.

[32] "A Watertight Watergate Future: Americans in a Post-American Age," *Antioch
Review*, summer 1975, p. 19.

neighborhood level.[33] "It's only politicians who are able to tell you you don't live in a community, you live in a nation," Hess said at the 1975 meeting of the World Future Society. "People should start paying attention to the only place they can have direct influence on the future, and that is in their own little community."

Encyclopaedia Britannica's editors recently asked 1,000 contributors to the encyclopaedia's new *(Britannica 3)* edition the question: As the nation approaches its 200th birthday, do you think that democracy as we know it will survive? More than 60 per cent of the respondents answered yes, although many predicted change. Indeed, the future of capitalism has been the subject of considerable debate and prediction in recent years, much of it pessimistic. "Can Capitalism Survive?" was the title of a *Time* magazine cover story in August 1975. In another analysis about the same time, Gurney Breckenfeld, an editor of *Fortune* magazine, wrote: "The way we are moving now, the private-enterprise system as we know it could well disappear in another 30 years."[34]

Difficulty of Making Reliable Economic Forecasts

However, a central lesson of recent years is that economic predictions cannot be trusted. "Economic forecasters have miscalled the swift turns in the volatile U.S. economy so often in recent years that the suspicion is taking root that something has gone amiss with orthodox theories about the way the economy actually operates," wrote Breckenfeld. In a similar vein, Saul Friedman, an economics reporter for Knight Newspapers, wrote in *Harper's:* "Not since the Great Depression...have so many prominent economists been so wrong so often."[35] And Robert Heilbroner, a political economist at the New School for Social Research in New York, told the 1975 annual meeting of the American Economic Association that "the great body of economists failed to predict the major trends of economic affairs over the past two decades."

Harvard Business Review recently asked its readers to answer a questionnaire on the subject of what society will be like in 1985. More than 1,800 replied, and they indicated that top corporate managers and other business people see America changing from a loose, individualistic society to a more tightly planned communal one. Respondents were asked to state their preference between two opposing ideologies, the first espousing

---

[33] See "Neighborhood Control," *E.R.R.*, 1975 Vol. II, pp. 785-804.

[34] "The Perilous Prospect of a Low-Growth Economy," *Saturday Review*, July 12, 1975, p. 40.

[35] "The Dismal Religion: Economics as Faith Healing," July 1975, p. 28.

the traditional American system of individualism, private property, free competition and limited government, and the second stressing the idea that community needs are more important than individual rights and the government should step in to make sure society's needs are met. Not surprisingly, 70 per cent said they preferred the traditional ideology and 62 per cent thought it still prevailed today. But 73 per cent thought that by 1985, the second ideology would dominate in this country. Moreover, while 70 per cent preferred the traditional system, only 60 per cent thought it could solve future problems better.[36]

Potential U.S. Role in the World

AMERICA'S FUTURE cannot be considered in isolation from the rest of the world. "In our day we face the danger that the old-fashioned nationalism (with its corollary isolationism) will become newly respectable," historian Daniel J. Boorstin wrote recently. "We are in danger of forgetting our oldest American tradition, that the nation exists for the sake of principles that can be shared.... In every generation we must once again declare our independence, while finding new ways to discover and declare our community with the world."[37]

"It seems clear to me," Professor Benjamin R. Barber of Rutgers has said, "that the next century cannot and will not be an American century. Indeed, it will not be a century that belongs to any nation. It will be a global century, which for the first time truly belongs to all nations and the people in them." Similarly, Professor Max Lerner of Brandeis University wrote in *Foreign Affairs:* "A hegemonial domination like the *Pax Romana*...has been made archaic by nuclear weapons, political warfare, the technology of instant communication, an interdependent global economy, and even the incipient rise of a world community of conscience."[38]

Pressures on the United States from other nations are certain to increase. There will be strong challenges from America's ideological enemies, strident demands from non-aligned nations

---

[36] William F. Martin and George Cabot Lodge, "Our Society in 1985—Business May Not Like It," *Harvard Business Review*, November-December 1975, p. 143.

[37] "America: Our Byproduct Nation," *Time*, bicentennial essay, June 23, 1975, p. 70.

[38] "America Agonistes," *Foreign Affairs*, January 1974, p. 289.

and urgent requests from American allies. Meanwhile, the crisis conditions that characterized much of the past few decades are likely to persist; some analysts predict a state of more or less "permanent revolution" around the world during the next century. "And this is a main reason for worry at America's 200th birthday," wrote Macrae in *The Economist*. "There is a danger that the Americans, with all their power for dynamism and good, may be about to desert what should be their manifest and now rather easy destiny of leading the rest of us towards a decent world society and an abundant cheap lunch. If they do, the leadership of the world may be yielded from American to less sophisticated hands, at a perilous moment."[39]

Recommendations are plentiful as to what policies should be followed. Robert O. Keohane of the Institute of Political Science at Stanford University has suggested that the nation renounce the use of force to control the internal development and non-military affairs of other countries; follow a policy of long-term interdependence with Europe and Japan; arrive at foreign policy decisions through a relatively open procedure instead of secret diplomacy; counter domestic opposition to internationalism by means of such devices as adjustment assistance payments to factories and workers hurt by imports; and recognize the need for radical change in much of the Third World.

Keohane's suggestions were made during a workshop at Harvard's Center for International Affairs in the summer of 1975. At the same gathering, Sidney Verba, a professor of government at Harvard, commented: "The possibility of the public playing a role in foreign policy is increased as the nature of the most important issue changes from security to economic." Robert Pittman of the *St. Petersburg* (Fla.) *Times*, who reported on the workshop, wrote (July 5, 1975) that behind most of the predictions made by participants lay an optimistic assumption: "It is that the global future is manageable. As complex and difficult as the issues will be, they are well within man's reach."

Today, however, the nation still seems to be floundering while it tries to settle on a new direction in international affairs. "We have lost, not our will, nor our might, but our compass," Stanley Hoffmann, professor of government and chairman of the Center for European Studies at Harvard University, said recently.[40] Hoffmann believes it is essential for Americans to understand three points: that the new world of the future may turn out to be totally unmanageable; that the United States is ill-equipped to try to control the uncontrollable; and that the American public, Congress and the executive branch must be prepared to face these new world realities.

[39] See *America's Changing World Role*, Editorial Research Reports book, 1974.
[40] "America Now: A Failure of Nerve?" *Commentary*, July 1975, p. 39.

Perhaps the most unpredictable factors in the equation of future U.S. foreign policy are the attitudes and actions of the so-called Third World countries—those not aligned with either Western or Communist nations. These slowly developing, overly populous and generally poor countries, most in the southern hemisphere, represent a potentially volatile force in global politics.

Rising Third World Resentment Toward the West

Food is one of the resources that many futurists believe will be in short supply in coming decades. World population is expected to climb to around seven billion by the year 2000, compared to about four billion today, and many experts question whether it will be possible to feed everyone. "I don't think we can reasonably expect to have the food supply go up sufficiently to feed those three billion as well as the four billion being fed now," Dr. Isaac Asimov, a leading futurist, has said: "I anticipate, in the course of the next 25 years, there will be a kind of famine psychology surrounding earth's population. I think the great, big, fat problem of the next 25 years is getting enough food."[41] Another fear is that global climate changes may affect the world food supply.[42]

William Paddock, an agricultural consultant and author of the forthcoming book *Time of Famine*, believes that frequent famines are inevitable and that the world will have to let people starve to death in societies that fail to cut their birth rates. Third World nations undoubtedly will not like this "solution" to world hunger and population problems. They would much prefer a radical redistribution of food and financial resources. "[T]he kinds of concessions that the Third World wants would require a significant restructuring of world markets, industries, and standards of living," *Business Week* commented in a recent issue. "What the Third World is really after is a widespread redistribution of income among nations: taking wealth from the rich industrialized countries and giving it to the poor underdeveloped countries."[43]

The gap between grinding poverty in much of the southern hemisphere and relative prosperity in much of the northern is probably the most urgent international issue for the future. The Overseas Development Council reports that the world's 42 poorest countries, with a population of about one billion, need an additional $4 billion in aid if they are to achieve an economic growth rate of 2 per cent a year through 1980. Some American

---

[41] Quoted by Louise Lague in *The Washington Star*, April 27, 1975. See "World Food Needs," *E.R.R.*, 1974 Vol. II, pp. 825-844.

[42] See "World Weather Trends," *E.R.R.*, 1974 Vol. II, pp. 515-538.

[43] "What the Third World Wants," *Business Week*, Oct. 13, 1975, p. 56.

leaders have indicated that the United States would be willing to participate in a new international economic order. Secretary of State Henry A. Kissinger, addressing a special session of the United Nations General Assembly on Sept. 1, 1975, said America was ready to help bring about major changes. The problem is primarily one of implementation. Daniel P. Moynihan, U.S. Representative to the U.N., has written: "We have no desire...to participate in a new economic arrangement whose beneficiaries will be the state rather than the individual, leaders rather than the individual, politicians and bureaucrats rather than the individual. If there is to be an increased flow of wealth to the countries of the South, the United States will insist that it be channeled into the pockets of individuals and not into Swiss bank accounts...."[44]

Possibilities of World Government or Nuclear War

Trends in international relations have led many to speculate that some kind of world government might evolve during the next 100 years. But this usually brings up the famous reply of Liaquat Ali Kahn, when he was Prime Minister of Pakistan, to the question whether he favored the idea of world government: "Do the supporters of the idea of world government realize," he replied, "that were it to happen it would neither be white, Christian, nor democratic?" Others believe that any potential world government almost certainly would be authoritarian, and probably would combine a kind of religious orientation with a militaristic discipline. "It is likely that China comes closest today to representing this new civilizational form," Robert Heilbroner has said.

Another frequent prediction for the next century is that a nuclear holocaust will occur, either as the superpowers push a confrontation over the brink or as small nations and terrorist groups acquire nuclear weapons. Members of a recent Harvard-MIT Arms Control Seminar concluded that nuclear war, in some form, will erupt before the end of the century. The panelists, who reported their conclusions in the November 1975 issue of *Harvard Magazine,* said that the other alternative is for the world to submit to an authoritarian international government which possesses nuclear weaponry. "A very nasty kind of world government may be necessary if we are to survive in the world I see ahead," said George Rathjens, an MIT professor. "Such a harsh government is a very grim prospect and it's not very likely. Nuclear war is more conceivable." Most of the panelists felt that the world's nations would face nuclear doomsday before surrendering their sovereignty.

[44] "America's Crisis of Confidence," *The New Leader,* Oct. 27, 1975, p. 13.

Planning for America's Future

P LANNING is a popular word today, as Americans of many persuasions call for studies of the nation's future and the development of policies which can better anticipate and respond to future change. At the World Future Society meeting in 1975, Professor Harold Linstone of Portland (Ore.) State University said that "truly long-range planning is no longer a luxury but a critical necessity." Many agree with this view, even though national planning—scorned by some as "social engineering"—long has been a dirty word in the United States.

Indeed, there is still widespread and potent resistance to national planning of any kind. Thomas A. Murphy, chairman of General Motors, has said, "National planning is a prescription for national chaos—or at best, national stagnation." And Charles Schultze of the Brookings Institution believes that "planning has become a sort of 'buzz word' that people seize on to avoid the hard political choices."[45] Most members of the U.S. economic establishment would prefer to tinker with the present system in the traditional fashion. Still, many believe that more planning is inevitable for America's future. Professor Otis Graham of the University of California at Santa Barbara, author of *Toward a Planned Society* (1975), has written: "At some point, the doubts about planning will appear less substantial than our doubts about the future under current governing arrangements, and the United States will then legislate planning in some form."[46]

The danger of long-range planning, some believe, is that it will necessitate a stronger centralized government. "Clearly the stage is being set for the imposition of grand designs upon man's future," said Jib Fowles of the University of Houston. Nonetheless, there are many who believe that more planning is essential if the nation is to survive the crises that lie ahead. Administrator Russell E. Train of the Environmental Protection Agency summed up these sentiments in a speech to the Conference Board last spring:

> [W]e all agree that this country must understand and accept the fact that the really critical issues before it are not the immediate and isolated ones, but the interrelated and long-range

[45] Quoted by Hobart Rowen, *The Washington Post,* Nov. 27, 1975.
[46] "Planning the Economy," *The Center Magazine,* November-December 1975, p. 58.

ones—indeed, the day-to-day 'crises' that seem to capture all our attention and consume all our energies are, for the most part, simply manifestations of far deeper problems that we never seem to get around to acknowledging, much less addressing.... Under these conditions we cannot hope to come to grips with the issues before us unless we strengthen our ability to assess problems and programs, not simply in isolation but in relation to each other; not simply over the short term but over the longer span of 10, 20 or 30 years.[47]

Question of Participation by Individual Citizens

The question is, who will do the extensive long-range planning for society if not a strong central government? There is considerable support for more public participation in future planning, but thus far it has not taken hold on any significant scale. Alvin Toffler, founder of the Ad Hoc Committee on Anticipatory Democracy, is optimistic that more citizens' futurist groups will spring up around the nation to help plan America's next century. "These organizations, spontaneously growing in all parts of the nation, suggest that the discussion of the nation's long-term options will not be limited to specialists but will come to involve very large sectors of the public," Toffler has predicted.

At the national level, several major planning proposals may soon come before Congress. Sen. Edward M. Kennedy (D Mass.) is drafting legislation to create a National Institute of Policy Analysis and Research, a kind of semi-autonomous think tank which would supply the legislative and executive branches with independent and objective analyses focusing on the future. Another Kennedy proposal is for an Experimental Futures Agency which would provide a national showcase for new technologies such as solar energy development; another measure would finance local Citizens Assessment Associations to help people address the major problems to be faced in years ahead.

In the economic realm, Sens. Hubert H. Humphrey (D Minn.) and Jacob Javits (R N.Y.) are co-sponsoring a bill, the "Balanced Growth and Economic Planning Act," which represents the first attempt at centralized national planning since the 1930s. It would create an economic planning board in the Executive Office of the President whose job would be to devise a long-range plan, to be reviewed every two years, to guide federal policy and inform private industry and local governments as to national goals. The board, with the help of a Cabinet-level council on economic planning and an advisory committee including citizen representatives, would establish criteria for monetary policy, unemployment housing and price controls.[48]

---

[47] "Planning to Take Charge of Our Future," *The Conference Board Record*, May 1975, p. 58.
[48] See *Congressional Quarterly Weekly Report*, Dec. 6, 1975, p. 2628.

Colonization of Space?

Some futurists believe the next frontier for humankind is outer space, and that colonization of space will help solve the earthly problems of overpopulation, resource depletion, energy shortages, pollution and economic troubles. Gerard K. O'Neill, a physics professor at Princeton University, believes that a permanent space station halfway between the earth and the moon could be built within 25 years. Solar energy would provide a free, inexhaustible power source for industry and agriculture, and the first colony could support a population of about 10,000.

O'Neill calculates that the station could be built at a cost comparable to the $33 billion Apollo moon program. Subsequent space stations could be constructed at much lower cost and eventually would colonize the solar system, using the moon, asteroids and other planets for raw materials.

Another economic planning proposal was developed by Gar Alperovitz and Jeff Faux of the Exploratory Project for Economic Alternatives and presented to the National Democratic Issues Convention in Louisville, Ky., in November 1975. This plan envisions a guaranteed job for every American, price controls on most consumer items, public ownership of major industries, employee ownership of business, and government controls over natural resources and capital. Although the plan resembles socialism, its supporters believe that Americans are ready for drastic changes in the traditional economic system. "Planning is no longer a negative word," said pollster Patrick Caddell, who reported that he had found strong public support for allocating national resources and breaking up large corporations that behave anticompetitively.[49]

The main question about planning for the future is whether the American public will be allowed to play a meaningful role. In the past, many argue, officials and institutions have conducted their affairs without adequate citizen participation. As a result, human values and social goals have not been considered fully in the decision-making process. Futurist Robert Jungk of the West Berlin Center for Future Research has said that "the man-on-the-street and his imagination are important in making the future."

There are no inevitabilities in the future, whether of disaster or utopia. But as America faces the decades ahead, individual Americans must see to it that the future becomes a central concern of ordinary citizens as well as decision-makers. That is perhaps the most difficult challenge of all for the nation as it begins its next century.

---

[49] *The New York Times*, Dec. 3, 1975.

Selected Bibliography

Books

Bell, Daniel, *The Coming of Post-Industrial Society*, Basic Books, 1973.

Clarke, Arthur C., *Profiles of the Future*, Harper & Row, 1958.

Ehrlich, Paul R. and Dennis C. Pirages, *Ark II: Social Response to Environmental Imperatives*, Viking, 1974.

Goodwin, Richard, *The American Condition*, Doubleday, 1974.

Hacker, Andrew, *The End of the American Era*, Atheneum, 1970.

Heilbroner, Robert, *An Inquiry Into the Human Prospect*, Norton, 1974.

Kahn, Herman and B. Bruce-Briggs, *Things to Come: Thinking About the Seventies and Eighties*, Macmillan, 1972.

Maddox, John, *The Doomsday Syndrome*, McGraw-Hill, 1972.

Meadows, Donella H., Dennis L. Meadows, Jorgen Randers, William W. Behrens III, *The Limits to Growth*, Universe Books, 1972.

Mesarovic, Mihajlo and Eduard Pestel, *Mankind at the Turning Point*, Dutton, 1974.

Muller, Herbert J., *Uses of the Future*, Indiana University Press, 1974.

Newman, Joseph, *1994: The World of Tomorrow*, U.S. News & World Report Books, 1973.

Theobald, Robert, *Futures Conditional*, Bobbs-Merrill, 1972.

Thompson, William Irwin, *At the Edge of History*, Harper & Row, 1972.

Toffler, Alvin, *Future Shock*, Random House, 1970.

Toynbee, Arnold, *Surviving the Future*, Oxford University Press, 1971.

World Future Society, *The Next 25 Years: Crisis and Opportunity*, 1975.

Articles

Boorstin, Daniel J., "America: Our Byproduct Nation," *Time*, June 23, 1975.

Breckenfeld, Gurney, "The Perilous Prospect of a Low-Growth Economy," *Saturday Review*, July 12, 1975.

Campbell, Colin and Robert Heilbroner, "Coming Apart at the Seams," *Psychology Today*, February 1975.

Clarke, Gerald, "Putting the Prophets in Their Place," *Time*, Feb. 15, 1971.

Conservation Foundation, "Futurists Call for Reforms in Planning," *Letter*, June 1975.

Cousins, Norman, "Prophecy and Pessimism," *Saturday Review/World*, Aug. 24, 1974.

Graham, Otis, "Planning the Economy," *The Center Magazine*, November-December 1975.

Holden, Constance, "Futurism: Gaining a Toehold in Public Policy," *Science*, July 11, 1975.

Lerner, Max, "America Agonistes," *Foreign Affairs*, January 1974.

Macrae, Norman, "America's Third Century: A Survey," *The Economist*, Oct. 25, 1975.

Martin, Jay, "A Watertight Watergate Future: Americans in a Post-American Age," *Antioch Review*, Summer 1975.

Martin, William F. and George Cabot Lodge, "Our Society in 1985—Business May Not Like It," *Harvard Business Review*, November-December 1975.

Schrag, Peter, "America Needs An Establishment," *Harper's*, December 1975.

Time, "Can Capitalism Survive?" Aug. 14, 1975.

Train, Russell E., "Planning to Take Charge of Our Future," *Conference Board Record*, May 1975.

Evaluating Presidential Performance

by

David Boorstin

Feb. 13
1 9 7 6

EVALUATING
PRESIDENTIAL PERFORMANCE

A S THE GEARS of another presidential campaign begin to grind in earnest, American voters start to formulate their ideas as to what makes a person fit for the most powerful elective post in the world. In their final decision, the candidate's political views and positions on various issues will be important. Just as important, however, will be the voters' views as to how the candidate's performance in office is likely to compare with that of his predecessors.

Evaluations of presidential performance are rarely constant, and the closer the performance is to our own day the more likely it is that current evaluations will change. "Whoever, in writing modern history, shall follow truth too near at the heels, it may haply strike out all his teeth," Sir Walter Raleigh warned in 1614.[1] In writing about Presidents this is a special danger, for the office is surrounded by an aura of quasi-religious sentimentality and respect. When a President appears successful, he becomes an idol; when his efforts fail, or if he proves incapable of living up to the presidential image, he is vilified.

Trying to judge a President's performance is also difficult because, in the words of historian Bert Cochran, "The modern presidency is not primarily a machine for self-expression.... [A President] is part of an intricate governmental and extra-governmental machinery so that what he is and is not able to do is more dependent on circumstances, contingencies, and interactions than on personal exercises of will and assertions."[2] At the same time, the fact remains that who the President is at any given time can make a profound difference in the nation's life.

The nation's bicentennial and the shocks of Watergate add significance to this November's ballot, and to the presidential primaries, caucuses and conventions which precede it. Presidential performance is the subject of new scrutiny, "for the new frustration and apathy aroused by Watergate have done much to dash and distort popular expectations of the presidency," wrote political scientist Thomas E. Cronin. "While on the one hand aspirations have crashed, on the other hand yearnings,

---

[1] Preface to his *History of the World*.
[2] Bert Cochran, *Harry Truman and the Crisis Presidency* (1973), pp. 120, 393.

sometimes feverish ones, have been rekindled for new candidates who are above politics and could somehow cleanse the office and elevate its performance to match the textbook portrait of the presidency."[3] In such an atmosphere it is both opportune and necessary to review the performance of some past Presidents, and to note the individual characteristics for which they now are hailed or condemned.

Retrospective Rise in Harry Truman's Popularity

One clear example of the fickleness of popular judgment is the wave of "Trumania" which has struck the United States in the recent past. Although *Time* magazine has noted[4] that "of recent Presidents, only Truman and Dwight Eisenhower...were able to retire from office with their reputations largely intact," Truman's popular reputation now appears to have reached new heights. Truman has become the subject of a successful theatrical production,[5] a television "special" on his stormy relations with Gen. Douglas MacArthur, and even a hit song by a rock band, which sings "Harry could you please come home?"[6] The number of tourists and researchers visiting the Truman library in Independence, Mo., is reported to have increased. Merle Miller's book of Truman reminiscences, *Plain Speaking*, enjoyed months on the best-seller lists and sold some 2.5 million copies. A personal biography by daughter Margaret Truman Daniel has also enjoyed success, and will be made into a film.

Simple nostalgia has played a part in this trend. But most observers trace Truman's new popularity to the effects of Watergate. His reputation for straightforwardness struck people of all ages as a refreshing contrast to revelations of political dishonesty in the Watergate era. Truman's portrait today is that of a folksy man who spoke his mind and maintained his salty character amidst the trappings of power. "Nobody could make him into a 'play-actor,' and I don't think it ever entered his mind to worry about his image," John P. Roche wrote in *Saturday Review/World*, Feb. 23, 1974.

It is perhaps ironic, then, that Truman's current appeal is as much a matter of style as of substance. President Ford had no hesitation in placing a bust of the Missouri Democrat in the Oval Office, nor in comparing himself to Truman—despite having criticized Truman's politics earlier in his career. "Truman, the most partisan of men, has become a saint for all parties," observed political journalist Garry Wills. "He even bridges the ideology gap."[7]

---

[3] Thomas E. Cronin, *The State of the Presidency* (1975), p. 26.
[4] June 9, 1975, p. 45.
[5] *Give 'Em Hell Harry!* featuring James Whitmore.
[6] "Harry Truman" by Chicago.
[7] "I'm Not Wild About Harry," *Esquire*, January 1976, p. 91.

The current spirit of admiration for Harry S Truman is in striking contrast to the opinions expressed of him during his administration. Although Truman entered the White House in 1945 on Franklin D. Roosevelt's death with a high popularity rating, as measured by the Gallup Poll, by 1951 his rating had fallen to the lowest of any President—23 per cent, one point lower than even Richard M. Nixon's worst score. After the striking, patrician character of Roosevelt, the new President ("Harry who?") appeared to many as "no more than a drab little party hack, a man soiled by his association with one of the most dismal political machines in American politics [Kansas City's Pendergast machine], devoid of historical vision and a rube to boot."[8] Commentator Walter Lippmann wrote, "How are the affairs of the country to be conducted by a President who not only has lost the support of his party but is not in control of his own administration?... Mr. Truman is not performing, and gives no evidence of his ability to perform, the functions of the Commander-in-Chief."[9]

While credited with carrying on Roosevelt's New Deal domestic programs, Truman now stands accused by some historians of ordering atomic bombs dropped on Japan to frighten Russia rather than to end a war which, they contend, was virtually won already.[10] Truman is also seen as an architect of the Cold War and its hysteria. Garry Wills wrote that Truman "put the nation in a state of permanent war

[8] Chilton Williamson Jr., "So in Love with Harry..." *The New Republic*, Feb. 9, 1974, p. 23.
[9] Quoted by James David Barber, *The Presidential Character* (1972), p. 279.
[10] An early advocate of that view was Gar Alperovitz in his *Atomic Diplomacy: Hiroshima and Potsdam* (1965). The same thesis was expounded by other "revisionist" historians of the 1960s. A more recent study with a similar view is *Meeting at Potsdam* (1975) by Charles L. Mee Jr. A book dealing with the same theme but more sympathetic to Truman is *A World Destroyed: The Atomic Bomb and the Grand Alliance* (1975) by Martin J. Sherwin.

mobilization, with all the paraphernalia of secrecy, censorship, the draft, rush mobilization of new weapons systems (beginning with the hydrogen bomb), and crisis indoctrination."

"What is surprising [Wills continued] is not so much that the excesses of McCarthyism occurred as that Truman is credited with opposing those excesses, to the exclusion of noticing that he supported the norm from which they arose."[11] Wills' criticism of Truman extends to the man's character as well: contrary to popular impressions, he asserts, Truman's style of spontaneity was a carefully cultivated myth. Such criticisms notwithstanding, it appears likely that Truman's enduring character will be that of the "average" man whose unexpectedly strong qualities enabled him to assume awesome powers and responsibilities.

Truman's successor, Dwight D. Eisenhower, is also being seen by some in a new light. Immensely popular as a war hero—the commander of victorious Allied forces in Europe in World War II—"Ike" radiated paternal benevolence. But his critics say he achieved little in office. The domestic problems of poverty, racial prejudice and urban decay which surfaced during the 1960s might, they say, have been dealt with a decade earlier by an activist President. By bringing Ngo Dinh Diem to power in Vietnam and supporting French efforts to maintain the status quo in Indochina, Eisenhower is said to have laid the foundations for the American involvement there, while his attitude toward Russia and China furthered the Cold War.[12]

But another view of Eisenhower has also emerged, contrasting with his portrayal as a passive, ineffectual figurehead. Murray Kempton, a prominent critic of Eisenhower during his presidency, in 1967 called him "the President most superbly equipped for truly consequential decision we may ever have had, a mind neither rash nor hesitant, free of the slightest concern for how things might look, indifferent to any sentiment, as calm when he was demonstrating the wisdom of leaving a bad situation alone as when he was moving to meet it on those occasions when he absolutely had to."[13]

The same lack of activism for which Eisenhower has been criticized now appears a virtue in the eyes of some. Garry Wills has praised Eisenhower for his restraint in foreign policy. "He didn't feel this need to show off his courage.... [H]e was a very good President because he was not imperial in his foreign attitudes. He was not an aggrandizer of executive power at

---

[11] In this regard, Truman has been criticized for, among other things, requiring federal employees to adhere to a loyalty program and for not staying the execution of Ethel and Julius Rosenberg as atomic spies. For background on Cold War internal-security measures, see Congressional Quarterly's *Congress and the Nation,* Vol. I (1965), pp. 1645-1670.

[12] For example, see Peter Lyon, *Eisenhower: Portrait of the Hero* (1974).

[13] "The Underestimation of Dwight D. Eisenhower," *Esquire,* September 1967, p. 109.

home."[14] Wills feels that history will come to share his estimate of Eisenhower.

New Look at Kennedy Era; Personal Disclosures

Strikingly different from the presidencies of Truman and Eisenhower was that of John Fitzgerald Kennedy. A youthful, wealthy, Harvard-educated Bostonian with graceful good looks, Kennedy brought an air of glamor and activism into the White House. Humor, intelligence and optimism were qualities for which he was noted. He was able to combine an impression of youthful idealism—expressed in such statements as "Ask not what your country can do for you, ask what you can do for your country"—with one of dynamic pragmatism, in a way which appealed to foreigners as well as many Americans.

The abrupt and tragic end to Kennedy's life has affected the scope of historical assessment. Whenever a President dies in office a wave of deep emotion sweeps across the country, making objective judgments all but impossible. Now that the immediacy of his death has faded, however, there is no doubt that his reputation has suffered severely. "The Kennedy myth made the Kennedy backlash inevitable," Pierre Salinger told an interviewer. "So it's fashionable today to say his presidency was a disaster."[15] Salinger, the former President's press secretary, did not concur in that judgment, however.

In a look at how textbooks treated Kennedy a decade after his assassination, John Berendt found that "the emotional outpouring that followed his assassination has given way...to a more balanced, sober view of what Kennedy actually stood for." He found Kennedy to be "rather coolly seen as a President of only medium importance. Overall, Kennedy is seen as a failure on the domestic front." In foreign matters, the schoolbooks credit Kennedy with creating the Peace Corps and succeeding in the Cuban missile crisis, Berendt noted, and he escapes criticism for Vietnam.[16]

At a different level of analysis, Kennedy's role in involving the United States in Vietnam is now the focal point for strong criticism. The journalist David Halberstam traced this process in his book *The Best and the Brightest* (1969). He wrote of "the irony...that John Kennedy, rationalist, pledged above all to rationality, should continue the most irrational of all major American foreign policies, that policy [of non-recognition] toward China..." Because "it was not coming to terms with

---

[14] Interviewed by Steve Forrester in the *Willamette Week*, Portland, Ore., Nov. 10, 1975, p. 11.

[15] Interviewed by Philip Nobile in *Midwest*, Chicago *Sun-Times* magazine, June 22, 1975, p. 5.

[16] "A Look at the Record," *Esquire*, November 1975, pp. 140, 263.

China, the Kennedy administration would soon expand the Eisenhower administration policy and commitment in Vietnam."

> He had preached [Halberstam continued] both in his book and in his speeches, about the importance of political courage, but his administration had been reasonably free from acts of courage, such as turning around the irrationality of the China policy. In this most crucial area the record was largely one of timidity.[17]

The Kennedy team's "cult of competence," summed up in the title of Halberstam's book, is portrayed as having resulted in mental arrogance—with terrible consequences for the nation.

The view of many analysts now is that while Kennedy's idealism was genuine, his pragmatism was misplaced. Chester Bowles, Under Secretary of State in the Kennedy administration, wrote in his personal notebook at the time: "The question which concerns me most about the new administration is whether it lacks a genuine sense of conviction about what is right and what is wrong."[18] Putting too high a premium on rationality, Bowles observed, may be dangerous in times of crisis when only fundamental moral beliefs can provide a President with clear and immediate direction. "The irony is that Kennedy overlooked moral perceptions as impractical," wrote Suzannah Lessard, "whereas it turns out they were profoundly pragmatic."

The Watergate scandals have added another dimension to this criticism of Kennedy. Lewis J. Paper, author of a recent book on that President, sees "an unmistakable connection between the habits of his presidency and the abuses of the Nixon presidency. Not that Kennedy's administration engaged in widespread illegal and unethical activities," he explains, "but many of the practices which blossomed in the Nixon administration and led to his downfall were implanted or nurtured during the Kennedy years."[19] In their zeal to achieve their goals, Paper argues, both Presidents were willing to use unconstitutional means. The lesson he draws is that "an attractive personality is no guarantee of good government; and a society that places its primary faith in the temperament of its leaders rather than in the wisdom of its procedures is courting disaster."

The very shortcomings of presidential character have emphasized the connection between personality and performance in office. One month before Nixon's resignation, Hugh

---

[17] *The Best and the Brightest* (1969), pp. 128-130, 368.
[18] Quoted by Suzannah Lessard in "A New Look at John Kennedy," *The Washington Monthly*, October 1971, p. 15.
[19] *The Washington Post*, Nov. 16, 1975, adapted from *The Promise and the Performance: The Leadership of John F. Kennedy* (1975).

Sidey observed in *Time:* "Almost all of our national political leaders are totally consumed by the pursuit and exercise of power.... Yet our best Presidents have clung to small pleasures that tied them to the ground and their fellow citizens." The rituals and the reality of presidential power "mean nothing unless there's a human dimension beneath and beyond the spectacle. And that is the continuing shadow across the restless trail of Richard Nixon."

The recent allegation that President Kennedy had a "close personal" relationship[20] with a woman who was also involved with Mafia figures released a flood of gossip about his private life which had been restrained during his administration. The revelations shocked some and amused others, depending on the connection they drew between public morality and private conduct. It was recalled that Thomas Jefferson, Warren G. Harding and Franklin Delano Roosevelt were rumored to have had mistresses at the White House,[21] while Grover Cleveland was the acknowledged father of an illegitimate child.

Identification of Presidential Personality Traits

An intriguing perspective on the relation between a man's deportment and his role as President was provided by Duke University political scientist James David Barber in his book *The Presidential Character: Predicting Performance in the White House* (1972). "*Before* a President is elected," Barber wrote, "debate centers on his stands on particular issues, his regional and group connections, his place in the left-right array of ideologies. *After* a President has left office and there has been time to see his rulership in perspective, the connection between his character and his presidential actions emerges as paramount."

Professor Barber's thesis is that the crucial differences between potential Presidents can be anticipated by an understanding of each individual's psychological makeup—his character, his world view and his style, which are established at different points in the man's life. Barber classifies presidential personality into four broad categories, defined according to (a) how active the man is and (b) whether or not he gives the impression he enjoys his political life:

> *Active-positive* Presidents have confidence in themselves and want most to achieve results. They enjoy their power, but are able to use it flexibly, "suiting the dance to the music," and to main-

---

[20] As characterized by Judith Campbell Exner, now a Southern California housewife who seeks to publish a book describing what she contends was a secret and social relationship with Kennedy while he was President. *Time* magazine, in reporting what she had already told the press, also wrote of "Jack Kennedy's Other Women" in its issue dated Dec. 29, 1975.

[21] See *Thomas Jefferson: An Intimate History* (1974) by Fawn N. Brodie, *Shadow of Blooming Grove: The One Hundred Years of Warren Gamaliel Harding* (1968) by Francis Russell, and *Eleanor and Franklin* (1971) by Joseph P. Lash.

tain a certain healthy detachment between themselves and their work. Barber puts Franklin D. Roosevelt, Harry S Truman and John F. Kennedy in this category.

Active-negative Presidents lack strong confidence in themselves, and suffer a contradiction between their intense effort in office and relatively low enjoyment of their work. These men seem ambitious and power-seeking, and their activity "has a compulsive quality, as if the man were trying to make up for something or to escape from anxiety into hard work." Woodrow Wilson, Herbert Hoover, Lyndon Johnson and Richard M. Nixon are seen this way.

Passive-positive Presidents are receptive and compliant, seeking affection as a reward for being agreeable and cooperative rather than personally assertive. The contradiction they suffer is between low self-esteem and an appearance of hopefulness and optimism. William Howard Taft and Warren G. Harding are offered as illustrations of Presidents who achieve little but enjoy the personal adulation of the presidency.

Passive-negative Presidents "are in politics because they think they ought to be." They do little and enjoy it less, tending to withdraw from the conflict and uncertainty of politics by emphasizing vague principles and procedural arrangements. While they can represent a "breathing spell" in the nation's political life, they also present the danger of drift. What passive Presidents ignore active Presidents inherit. Calvin Coolidge was of this type, according to Barber.

To establish this new framework for evaluating Presidents, Barber dug deeply into the childhood and early political experience of his subjects. For the active-negative Presidents, especially, Barber found significant policy failures rooted in their characters. Johnson and Nixon, confronted with growing crises, both showed a "process of rigidification, a movement from political dexterity to narrow insistence on a failing course of action despite abundant evidence of failure." Although Barber, writing in 1972, noted Nixon's first term had been generally moderate and flexible, he saw clues that a second-term Nixon, like the second-term Wilson or post-1965 Johnson, might show a very different face of power.

Barber's analysis appears to have stood as a successful prediction of Nixon's reaction to the Watergate crisis two years later: "The danger is that crisis will be transformed into tragedy—that Nixon will go from a dramatic experiment to a moral commitment, a commitment to follow his private star, to fly off in the face of overwhelming odds. That type of reaction is to be expected when and if Nixon is confronted with a severe threat to his power and sense of virtue."

Whether Barber's views will enable voters in 1976 to choose the best possible President is doubtful. Bill Moyers, a former White

House assistant to Johnson, commented in a review of the book, "We can't know 'the man whole,' and, even if we did, we would likely be just as prone to vote as much by gut feel as anything."[22] Barber does succeed, however, in emphasizing the importance of personality in presidential performance and the value, if not the feasibility, of applying psychological analysis to those who would be President.

Past Views of the Presidential Role

A MERICA WON its independence without a President. The Continental Congress had both legislative and executive power. Experience with this plan of government led the republic's founders to favor more centralization of executive authority. At the same time, their experience with King George III made them careful to limit the powers of the executive. The unique American solution was to create an office that was both head of state and head of government answerable to the legislature: less than a king but more than a prime minister.

Those Founding Fathers who feared the establishment of a tyranny were reassured by the presence of George Washington and the expectation that he would be the first to fill the new position. Englishman James Bryce (Viscount Bryce) observed in his classic two-volume study of American institutions, *The American Commonwealth* (1901):[23] "The creation of the office would seem justified by the existence of a person exactly fitted to fill it, one whose established influence and ripe judgment would repair the faults then supposed to be characteristic of democracy, its impulsiveness, its want of respect for authority, its incapacity for pursuing a consistent line of action."

From its inception, the nature of the office was strongly affected by the character and reputation of the man who held it. George Washington—a "passive-negative" President in Barber's terms—sought stability rather than action, and by his nature helped to establish the legitimacy of the new American government.

Furthermore, the Washington legend has continued to have its effect on the way Americans regard the nation's highest office. The newly independent colonies had a need for a common history—mythical as well as factual—to bind them together. "A measure of their success," historian Daniel J. Boorstin wrote, "is

---

[22] "What Manner of Man in the Big White House?" *Saturday Review,* Aug. 5, 1972, p. 50.
[23] Third edition, revised from the 1888 original edition.

how much has been popularly forgotten of the true story of George Washington, especially in his later years."

> Few remember that Washington had more than his share of enemies, that for all his life he was a controversial figure, and that during his presidency he was personally libeled with a venom aimed at few of his successors.... Not only his judgment but his integrity had been publicly impugned.... But he was destined to a stature in death which he had never attained in life.[24]

Mason Lock Weems, an Anglican clergyman better known as Parson Weems, was the first of a long line of biographers credited with creating the Washington legend. From 1808 onward, *Weems's Life of George Washington: With Curious Anecdotes, Equally Honorable to Himself and Exemplary to His Young Countrymen* went through 20 editions and became a best-seller of its day. To fact Weems added materials borrowed, stolen, or invented, including the famous story of the cherry tree: "I can't tell a lie, Pa; you know I can't tell a lie. I did cut it with my hatchet." Through fact and fable, Weems and his successors built an awesome legend for future Presidents to be measured against.

Denunciations of Lincoln's Civil War Presidency

Today Abraham Lincoln shares with Washington the honor of embodying all that is seen as right and good in a President. An analytical poll taken in 1968 which considerably enlarged the Schlesinger polls of 1948 and 1962 *(see box, p. 37)* showed that among historians Lincoln ranked first in accomplishments in office, while in strength of action they considered him surpassed by only Franklin D. Roosevelt.[25] The historians ranked Lincoln over Washington and every other President in general prestige. Yet during his administration, Lincoln was vilified in picture and in print in a manner which makes the libels on other Presidents appear mild by comparison.

The press in Lincoln's time provided a new and bigger forum for his virulent critics. "Washington seems to have been exempt from the attacks of caricaturists," Albert Shaw wrote in his Lincoln biography[26] in 1929, "but this was due to the lack of artists and engravers, rather than to respect for the man or the office." Shaw pointed out that "Lincoln drawn by cartoonists of the present time is always beneficent and dignified, making an appeal to our feelings of regard and veneration. Nothing could be

---

[24] Daniel J. Boorstin, *The Americans: The National Experience* (1965), pp. 338-339.

[25] Poll by historian Gary M. Maranell of 571 historians, originally published in *American History*, June 1970, reprinted in *Presidential Style* (1976) by Samuel and Dorothy Rosenman, pp. 552-555. It is interesting to note that the same poll rated both Lincoln and FDR as being far more practical than idealistic, while Wilson was seen as being far more idealistic than any other President.

[26] *Abraham Lincoln: His Path to the Presidency.*

Presidential Ratings

In 1948, Harvard Professor Arthur Schlesinger Sr. asked for the views of 55 experts on all the Presidents from Washington through Franklin D. Roosevelt. In 1962 the Schlesinger poll was expanded to 75 experts, who rated all the Presidents through Eisenhower.

While the poll offers an interesting perspective on presidential performance, it is worth noting what historian Bert Cochran wrote in his biography of President Truman, *Harry Truman and the Crisis Presidency* (1973): "To think...that it's possible to say something meaningful about American history and national administration by grading Presidents, like term papers, is to sink into scholastic fatuity [and]...to reduce history to a parlor game."

1962 Schlesinger Poll of Presidential Greatness

Great	*Average*	*Below Average*
1. Lincoln	12. Madison	24. Taylor
2. Washington	13. J. Q. Adams	25. Tyler
3. F. D. Roosevelt	14. Hayes	26. Fillmore
4. Wilson	15. McKinley	27. Coolidge
5. Jefferson	16. Taft	28. Pierce
	17. Van Buren	29. Buchanan
Near Great	18. Monroe	
	19. Hoover	*Failure*
6. Jackson	20. Harrison	
7. T. Roosevelt	21. Arthur	30. Grant
8. Polk) tie	22. Eisenhower) tie	31. Harding
9. Truman)	23. A. Johnson)	
10. John Adams		
11. Cleveland		

in greater contrast than the cartoons of his own lifetime." Cartoonists at home and abroad portrayed Lincoln as a moron, a lunatic and a bloody tyrant destroying the principles of American freedom.

Reasons for Lincoln's unpopularity in his own day are not hard to find. Racial hatred turned to hatred of Lincoln in the North as well as in the South. And there was the problem of presidential war powers. Arthur M. Schlesinger Jr. has written that Lincoln, in his attempt to save the nation, "ignored one law and constitutional provision after another." Lincoln enlarged the Army and Navy beyond their authorized strength, spent public money without congressional appropriation, suspended *habeas corpus*, instituted a naval blockade of the Confederacy and took other unprecedented steps—all unauthorized, for there had been no declaration of war by Congress. "Throughout the war, even with Congress in session, Lincoln continued to exercise wide powers independently of Congress."[27]

Today the almost-dictatorial powers assumed by Lincoln appear justified by the crisis which the nation faced. This is true, in part, because the Civil War established principles which were to prove relevant in evaluating other Presidents' responses to emergencies. Certain challenges to the country's very survival, it became evident, can only be met by a lowering of constitutional barriers against omnipotent government; and the President alone can provide the unity, leadership and decisive action necessary to deal with such crises. Later Presidents have been prepared to resort to extraconstitutional authority when they considered it necessary to the defense of the nation. But their performance in such extraordinary circumstances is ultimately judged by the manner in which they exercised such authority, and the genuineness of the threat.

"While Lincoln assumed extraordinary power, he always exercised it with utmost self-restraint, especially when individual liberty was involved," political scientist Robert S. Hirschfield wrote in 1971. "It was painful for him to violate the principles in which he believed....Both Wilson and Roosevelt might have averted the worst aspects of their crisis governments had they emulated Lincoln in his insistence that emergency power be used to circumscribe individual liberty only in cases of absolute necessity."[28] What distinguished Lincoln's performance as well, Hirshfield said, was the honesty with which he acknowledged the extraconstitutional nature of his crisis government, and the dangers inherent in emergency rule.

Ebb and Flow of Presidential Power in History

The congressional reaction to Lincoln's expansion of presidential powers reveals another factor to be accounted for in evaluating executive performance. Schlesinger wrote: "Nearly every President who extended the reach of the White House provoked a reaction toward a more restrictive theory of the presidency, even if the reaction never quite cut presidential power back to its earlier level."[29] Thus it was no accident that for 20 years after Lincoln—that is, until the election of Grover Cleveland in 1884—there was no strong President; and that the three Presidents following Wilson (Harding, Coolidge and Hoover) were similarly weak. Emergency presidential prerogatives were revived by Franklin D. Roosevelt, but in the

---

[27] Arthur M. Schlesinger Jr., *The Imperial Presidency* (1973), p. 58. See also "War Powers of the President," *E.R.R.*, 1966 Vol. I, pp. 192-193.

[28] "Lessons of Lincoln's 'Dictatorship,' " *The New York Times*, Feb. 12, 1971.

[29] Schlesinger, *op. cit.*, p. 68.

Lincoln Viewed in His Own Time

John Tenniel in Punch, Dec. 3, 1864

face of strong—and sometimes successful—congressional opposition. Unlike Lincoln, FDR did not exert his powers fully until
after the congressional declaration of war following the attack
on Pearl Harbor.

Roosevelt's presidency, combined with instances of congressional shortsightedness, led to what has been called the "cult
of the activist presidency" which shaped the minds of many in
the postwar generation. In the following decades the conflict
between congressional and presidential supremacy—especially
in foreign policy matters—was given new urgency by the image
of one man's finger pushing the button that would trigger a
holocaust. Increasingly, Presidents are judged by the degree to
which they controlled events or were victimized by them.

But to some extent every President is at the mercy of broad
historic currents, especially the phase of the congressional-
presidential conflict at the time he is in office. The same
President who could perform adequately in a period of relative

quiet and congressional dominance will be viewed less kindly if he is serving when the country faces emergencies and activism is called for. Such circumstances and events affect not only his performance in office but the way in which historians later regard him.

George E. Reedy, who served in the White House under Lyndon B. Johnson, observed that "Presidents glory in telling people that they are prisoners of a system and of circumstances beyond their control." Reedy, registering his dissent, wrote: "This is probably the subconscious device by which the chief executive prepares his alibi for history. It is true that they must deal with forces and circumstances which they did not create and which they cannot ignore. But how they deal with them is up to the Presidents themselves. A President, in a peculiar sense that does not apply to other people, is the master of his own fate and the captain of his own soul."[30]

The President's own personality helps determine how he will react to events. According to Joseph A. Califano Jr., who also served in the Johnson White House: "Personality is often decisive to the style in which presidential power is exercised."

> Eisenhower's staff system was military; his appearance fatherly. Kennedy's staff system was less structured; his appearance exuberant and energetic. Johnson's staff system was frenetic, seeking a cure for every ill; his appearance one of indefatigable perpetual motion, in constant conversation and consultation. Nixon's staff system was elaborately structured; his personal style one of lonely contemplation and suspicion, speaking to an unprecedently small number of aides.[31]

The preeminence of personality in American presidential politics is often decried, for it is said to distract attention from hard issues. Nonetheless it is impossible to ignore the ways in which a President's personality, as much as his political commitments, moves him to define the issues which are important to him and the approach he intends to take.

Evaluation of Presidential Candidates

IN A COUNTRY where political life is active and there is much emphasis on the free rise of talent, why have not more great men become President? Lord Bryce, writing at the turn of the century, remarked on this puzzling fact: "[S]ince the heroes of the Revolution died out with Jefferson and Adams and

---

[30] George E. Reedy, *The Twilight of the Presidency* (1970), p. 31.
[31] Joseph A. Califano Jr., *A Presidential Nation* (1975), p. 242.

Madison...no person except General Grant has reached the chair whose name would have been remembered had he not been President, and no President except Abraham Lincoln has displayed rare or striking qualities in the chair. Who now knows or cares to know anything about the personality of James K. Polk or Franklin Pierce? The only thing remarkable about them is that being so commonplace they should have climbed so high."[32]

Seventy-five years later, *Time* magazine asked its readers, "Can anyone remember when he last went to vote for a U.S. President and felt both enthusiastic and confident? Totally enthusiastic about his own candidate; reasonably confident that if his man lost, the other fellow would still be a good President? ...Between now and next November it is certain that the question will be asked again, often in anger: Out of our large (214 million) and highly educated population, is this the best choice the American system can offer?"[33]

Bryce discerned a number of reasons for this dismaying trend, most of them still recognized today by observers of the American political scene. No tradition of a leisured social class with time for statesmanship existed in this country as it did in parts of Europe. Much of America's best talent for thought and action, for planning and for executing was attracted into the business of developing the country's resources. The very breadth of this field—and its rewards—meant that persons were attracted to it who in other countries might have found their outlet in politics. Thus, Bryce observed, great men were rare to begin with in American politics.

Safety vs. Brilliance in Selection of Candidates

Just as fundamental is the observation that the method in which Presidents are chosen—first of all, as candidates—is not designed to bring men of stature to the top. Brilliant men are likely to have made enemies as well as admirers; and while party feeling may be enough to carry a person into office without conspicuous virtues, it may not do so if he has conspicuous faults.

Furthermore, the selection of a candidate involves considerations in addition to those of personal merit. The support of different states or sections of the country, politicking within the party, and the recognition of public prejudice all play their part. If the result is mediocrity, Bryce observed, "the ordinary American voter does not object to mediocrity.... He likes his candidate to be sensible, vigorous, and above all, what he calls 'magnetic,' and does not value, because he sees no need for, originality or profundity, a fine culture or a wide knowledge."

---

[32] *The American Commonwealth*, Vol. I, p. 78.
[33] "New Places to Look for Presidents," *Time*, Dec. 15, 1976.

If the safe candidate is to be preferred to the risky but distinguished one, that does not mean that the entire campaign effort is not designed to make a presidential candidate appear the greatest of all things to all people. And especially in a time when the same goals are shared by both parties, and there is no dramatic divergence in their approach to political issues, personality comes to the forefront. What Bryce noted three-quarters of a century ago still holds true: that in European countries elections turn chiefly on the views of the parties and only secondarily on the character of individual leaders, but that in America the two factors are confused. Perhaps most distressing of all is the fact that what makes a good candidate is not necessarily what makes a good President. Political qualities and executive qualities are not always the same—some would even argue they are mutually exclusive.

Changing Styles in Appeal of Presidential Candidates

In analyzing the performance of Presidents, it is worth examining the ways in which campaign managers seek to make their candidate look as if he would be a good President. While they cannot be said always to portray the true nature of their man scrupulously, campaign managers try to reflect the popular American attitude toward what a President should be. In some respects, Americans have never made up their minds as to what qualifies a person to be President.

In terms of political experience, the pattern has been a changing one: since John F. Kennedy's election in 1960, senators have dominated presidential campaigns. In the three succeeding races, every nominee of the two major parties was a senator or former senator, although this year two ex-governors (Ronald Reagan and Jimmy Carter) and a House member (Morris K. Udall) are contenders. In the 36 years before the Kennedy election, the two major parties nominated only one man who had ever served in the Senate—Harry S Truman, who was already President when nominated. The earliest tradition developed around the Secretary of State, considered the preeminent Cabinet officer and thus the most important person in the executive branch after the President."[34] In the first half of this century, the governor's office was the stepping-stone to the presidency for Theodore Roosevelt, Wilson, Coolidge and FDR. Harding had been a lieutenant governor. Their defeated rivals included Charles Evans Hughes, James M. Cox, Alfred E. Smith, Alfred Landon, and Thomas E. Dewey, governors all.

The changes in some positive presidential attributes can be seen in campaign literature over the years. Historian W. Burlie

---

[34] Secretaries of State who became Presidents were Thomas Jefferson, James Madison, James Monroe, John Quincy Adams, Martin Van Buren and James Buchanan. See *Congressional Quarterly Weekly Report*, Jan. 17, 1976, pp. 93-95.

Brown traced some of these in his study of the presidential image in campaign biographies.[35] After 1860, for example, Brown detected more emphasis on making the candidate an athlete and exploiting his love for children. Especially notable has been the part played by a candidate's military record.

In the 1970s, with memories of World War II fading and those of Vietnam still fresh, a candidate's war record appears to have little appeal. Today, however, television has created new requirements for those in politics. John F. Kennedy is widely hailed as having been the first great "media candidate," with good looks and a speaking style well suited to television. His success in the televised debates with Richard Nixon during the 1960 campaign is said by some to have won that close election.[36] Television's probing eye has made a good physical appearance more important than ever before to those who wish to appear as presidential material.

Enduring Qualities Valued by American Public

Perhaps even more important than the shifts in public attitudes are the constant qualities. Brown wrote in 1960: "One cannot fail to be struck by the essential similarity in so many respects of all of the candidates as they appeared in campaign biographies" since 1824. He found these unchanging characteristics so pervasive that he was able to draw a biographical sketch of "the perennial, the enduring candidate...that seemingly would have as much appeal to the voter of Jackson's day as to the voter of today."[37]

Such a candidate would have northern European ancestors who fought tyranny in the Old World, were early settlers in America and served the revolutionary cause in 1776. The young candidate was raised according to his parents' views of patriotism and Christian piety. Through education and hard work he rose above the humble circumstances of his birth. His successful career was interrupted briefly but gloriously by the call to defend his country. He then resumed his struggle to the top, which included stints as a farmer, lawyer and businessman, while offering service to the community which demanded his talents.

It is an image which in fact might not have fitted more than a handful of Presidents. Whether a President lives up to that campaign image of ideal First Citizen of the Republic, only history can judge. History's judgment of a President, it is worth remembering, is also a judgment of the country he leads.

---

[35] *The People's Choice: The Presidential Image in Campaign Biography* (1960).
[36] See *"Television and Politics," E.R.R.*, 1968 Vol. I, pp. 361-384.
[37] W. Burlie Brown, *op. cit.*, p. 144.

Selected Bibliography

Books

Barber, James David, *The Presidential Character: Predicting Performance in the White House*, Prentice-Hall, 1972.

Brown, W. Burlie, *The People's Choice: The Presidential Image in the Campaign Biography*, Louisiana State University Press, 1960.

Bryce, James, *The American Commonwealth* (2 vols.), Macmillan, 1901, third edition.

Califano, Joseph A. Jr. *A Presidential Nation*, W. W. Norton & Co., 1975.

Cronin, Thomas E. *The State of the Presidency*, Little, Brown & Co., 1975.

Halberstam, David, *The Best and the Brightest*, Random House, 1969.

Laski, Harold J., *The American Presidency: An Interpretation*, Harper & Bros., 1940.

Reedy, George E., *The Twilight of the Presidency*, World Publishing Co., 1970.

Rosenman, Samuel and Dorothy, *Presidential Style: Some Giants and a Pygmy in the White House*, Harper & Row, 1976.

Rossiter, Clinton, *The American Presidency*, Harcourt, Brace & World, 1960.

Schlesinger, Arthur M. Jr., *The Imperial Presidency*, Houghton Mifflin, 1973.

Articles

"The American Presidency," *Current History*, June 1974.

Berendt, John, "A Look at the Record," *Esquire*, November 1973.

"Everyone's Wild About Harry," *Newsweek*, March 24, 1975.

Cochran, Bert, "The Man Who Succeeded Roosevelt," *The Nation*, March 2, 1974.

Harris, Richard, "Reflections: Nixon and Lincoln," *The New Yorker*, April 15, 1974.

Johnson, Gerald W., "Truman Nostalgia," *The New Republic*, May 31, 1975.

Kempton, Murray, "The Underestimation of Dwight D. Eisenhower," *Esquire*, September 1967.

Lessard, Suzannah, "A New Look at John Kennedy," *The Washington Monthly*, October 1971.

Roche, John P., "Truman on Tape," *Saturday Review/World*, Feb. 23, 1974.

Sherrill, Robert, "Thank You Mama, We'll Be Careful About Him," *The Nation*, July 10, 1972.

"Trumania in the '70s," *Time*, June 9, 1975.

Wills, Garry, "I'm Not Wild About Harry," *Esquire*, January 1976.

Reports and Studies

Editorial Research Reports, "War Powers of the President," 1966 Vol. II, p. 181; "Credibility Gaps and the Presidency," 1968 Vol. I, p. 81; "American History: Reappraisal and Revision," 1969 Vol. II, p. 815; "Television and Politics," 1968 Vol. I, p. 361.

AMERICAN GLOBAL STRATEGY

by

Mary Costello

**Feb. 6
1976**

AMERICAN GLOBAL STRATEGY

T HREE YEARS after the U.S. withdrawal from Indochina, many Americans seem concerned that their country's power and prestige in the world is declining and that the Soviet Union is emerging as the dominant superpower. This concern has given rise to a debate about America's global strategy in the post-Vietnam era. Some insist that there is no consistent strategy and that the United States merely reacts to world crises. Others contend that détente, or relaxation of tensions between the two superpowers, is only a slightly more sophisticated version of the old containment-of-communism doctrine. Still others argue that détente is a dangerous and one-sided American effort that gives the Soviets what they could not otherwise obtain.

To those worried about America's global policy, the U.S. position in the world might be summarized as follows: "The United States cannot afford another decline like that which has characterized the past decade and a half. Fifteen years more of a deterioration of our position in the world...would find us reduced to Fortress America in a world in which we had become largely irrelevant. Our leadership is being questioned even by our allies....Periods of so-called flexibility identified with personal diplomacy ended with American prestige at an unprecedented low."

Ironically, those words were written 15 years ago by Henry A. Kissinger in his book *The Necessity for Choice* (1961). Many of the same criticisms that Kissinger directed at American foreign policy after World War II are now falling on the Secretary of State's personalized conduct of world affairs. His policy of détente with the Soviet Union, it is said, has led to a deterioration in U.S. relations with traditional allies and has done little to encourage Russian restraint.

The fragility of détente has become apparent in the civil war in Angola. The United States has funneled millions of dollars in military equipment to two anti-Communist factions while the Soviet Union is supporting a third group with arms, technicians and Cuban soldiers. The Ford administration has explained this country's covert intervention in Cold War fashion. American passivity in the fact of Soviet expansionism, President Ford and

Public Expectations of American Power

Americans have been asked repeatedly at year-end by Gallup pollsters if they thought each coming year would bring an increase or decrease in U.S. global power. Their views since 1960, together with the views of foreigners for 1976, are shown below:

American Views

For the year	Increase	Decline	Don't Know
1976	42%	44%	14%
1974	29	50	21
1969	62	21	17
1965	64	19	17
1960	72	10	18

Foreign Views—1976

Country	Increase	Decline	Don't Know
Chile	47%	22%	31%
India	38	15	47
West Germany	35	26	39
Great Britain	30	27	43
Canada	29	31	40
Sweden	23	30	47
Japan	12	13	75

Kissinger have argued, could tempt Kremlin leaders to intervene elsewhere and might convince allied and neutralist nations that the United States was no longer reliable.

Kissinger has repeatedly said that U.S. assistance to Angola was undertaken to prevent the imposition of a Soviet-backed regime against the wishes of the majority of Angolans and is in no way analogous to American intervention in Vietnam in the early 1960s. The Senate, unconvinced, voted Dec. 19 to cut off funds for Angola. Despite pleas from the administration, the House gave final approval to the cutoff, Jan. 27, by the lopsided margin of 323 to 99. Two days later, Kissinger said that the administration was considering a request for overt assistance to the anti-Communist factions in Angola. Few observers expect that Congress would be receptive to such a proposal.

The Angola vote was the latest in a series of recent attempts by Congress to reassert its role in foreign policy and, often, to indicate its opposition to Kissinger's handling of world affairs. Congress has in the past few years refused administration requests for aid to South Vietnam, insisted on a total and then a partial embargo on arms deliveries to Turkey, started reassessing the military sales program, inquired into Middle East policy, and conducted hearings on Central Intelligence Agency (CIA) secret operations abroad. In October 1975, the Senate Foreign Relations Committee began hearings, due to be concluded in May, on U.S. foreign policy goals. Witnesses include a wide variety of present and former government officials, foreign affairs analysts, journalists and others.

The committee is considering two seemingly paradoxical aspects of U.S. global strategy: pursuit of détente with the Soviet Union and efforts in the rest of the world to contain communism or other far-left advances. The first is a pragmatic policy while the second is grounded in Cold War ideology. This seeming dichotomy in foreign policy results from Kissinger's desire to achieve a "stable" international order.

Stability in the nuclear age requires peaceful competition and reduced tension between established superpowers. But stability could be endangered if countries like Angola or Chile came under Communist sway. Hans J. Morgenthau, the University of Chicago foreign-affairs scholar, offers this interpretation: "...[T]he United States can afford to play down ideological differences in its relations with the major Communist powers, for these differences do not affect the overall world balance of power. But it must take ideological advances and retreats at the confines of the two empires [Russian and American] with utmost seriousness."[1]

Criticism of U.S. foreign policy touches both its ideological and pragmatic aspects. Liberals, generally supportive of détente, tend to look upon American involvement in Angola and support for repressive but anti-Communist regimes as morally bankrupt and counter to long-term national interests. Conservatives argue that détente is an illusion, based more on wishful thinking than on the hard realities of Soviet duplicity. The price of détente is too great, they assert, when the President refuses to see the exiled Russian dissident Alexander Solzhenitsyn[2] and the United States sells grain to the Soviet Union at below-market prices.[3] What, they ask, has the United States gotten in return?

Conservatives have become even more skeptical of détente in recent months. They noted that the Soviet Union intervened in Angola despite warnings from Ford and Kissinger that intervention would jeopardize détente and perhaps wreck the chances for

---

[1] Hans J. Morgenthau, "Three Paradoxes:Explaining the Failure of U.S. Foreign Policy," *The New Republic*, Oct. 11, 1975, p. 16. Morgenthau is a professor of political science and history at the University of Chicago.

[2] When the Nobel Prize laureate visited Washington in June 1975, giving a speech critical of détente, President Ford did not invite him to the White House. Presidential aides said Ford was too busy and, moreover, preferred "substantive" meetings to "symbolic" ones.

[3] See "World Grain Trade," *E.R.R.*, 1973 Vol. II, p. 711.

obtaining a new treaty to limit strategic arms. Despite the apparent lack of any Soviet assurances that Moscow would end its support for the Marxist faction in Angola, Ford said on Jan. 5 that he would not withhold U.S. grain shipments to Russia in retaliation. Kissinger met with Kremlin leaders in Moscow later in the month for talks on an arms agreement.

Criticism of Kissinger Policy Toward U.S.S.R.

Former Secretary of Defense James R. Schlesinger has emerged as a spokesman for the so-called hard line in negotiations with the Russians on strategic arms. In an interview published in *U.S. News & World Report* on Dec. 22, 1975, Schlesinger expressed concern about American concessions in the 1972 SALT I agreements and the possibility of further concessions in SALT II. "For us to imply that Soviet adventures in Angola are sufficiently serious to endanger détente but treat alterations in the military balance so casually or as a mere bagatelle, strike me as ironical." Schlesinger's public insistence on higher defense spending and his undisguised differences with Kissinger over détente were assumed to be the reasons that Ford dismissed him from the defense post on Nov. 2.

Schlesinger has pointed to possible Soviet violations of the 1972 Strategic Arms Limitation Treaty (SALT I) and warned that the United States must not make further concessions in the SALT II talks now in progress. These views are shared by Sen. Henry M. Jackson (D Wash.), Ronald Reagan and George C. Wallace, all presidential contenders, and by AFL-CIO President George Meany and retired Adm. Elmo M. Zumwalt Jr., former chief of naval operations. Jackson, long a leading foe of détente, not only contends that the Russians violated the 1972 SALT agreement but he criticizes the drafting of the treaty. Its terms, he has said, "are so ill-defined, the loopholes so numerous, the ambiguities so exploitable that one would have to go out of one's way to 'violate' the few precise terms about which a definitive judgment might be made."

Kissinger denies that the United States has ignored possible Soviet violations of the letter or the spirit of the 1972 accords. It stands to reason, he said at a news conference in Washington on Dec. 9, 1975, "that the United States would not accept noncompliance with an agreement that had any conceivable impact on the strategic equation." The Secretary also charged that the allegation of Soviet non-compliance "may tempt the very noncompliance it seeks to avoid" by giving the impression that U.S. officials would "collude in a violation" of the agreement.

In an analysis of Kissinger's writings and speeches, Professor James E. Dornan Jr. has summed up the Secretary of State's policy on strategic weapons as follows: "Beyond a certain level the numbers and characteristics of nuclear weapons in a nation's arsenal are 'strategically insignificant.' " Such a view, Dornan said, "explains Kissinger's acceptance at SALT I of Soviet superiority in numbers of ICBMs and SLBMs...."[4] What matters to Kissinger "is the conclusion of agreements with the U.S.S.R. which add to the 'momentum of détente.' "[5]

A lack of momentum is evident in the delay in reaching a SALT II agreement. It was widely expected that a pact would be signed soon after President Ford and Soviet Party Chairman Leonid I. Brezhnev reached an agreement in Vladivostok in November 1974. Unlike SALT I, the Vladivostok agreement established exact equivalence between the superpowers in numbers of strategic weapons. But negotiations soon bogged down over a number of technical matters and particularly over the inclusion of the U.S. cruise missile and the Soviet Backfire bomber. In November 1975, a year after the heads-of-state meeting, the Russians rejected an American proposal to bring both weapons into the agreement. Kissinger responded by insisting that the next move was up to the Soviets.

Those convinced that the United States has given too much and gotten too little in return in past agreements with the Soviet Union are insisting that any American concessions—in SALT or trade, for example—be matched by Russian concessions in other areas. There was pressure on Kissinger during his trip to Moscow in January 1976 to use the so-called bargaining chip strategy by insisting that any American agreement on strategic arms be linked with a Soviet pledge to refrain from further involvement in Angola.

In at least one instance in the past, the bargaining chip strategy failed. The Foreign Trade Act of 1974 contained an amendment sponsored by Sen. Jackson to make the lowering of trade barriers with Russia—which the Kremlin sought—contingent upon its willingness to let more Russian Jews emigrate. Russian leaders reacted angrily to that stipulation and nullified the 1972 U.S.-Soviet trade agreement. The number of Jews permitted to leave Russia declined.

National Interest Outside Superpower Context

Détente outside the direct U.S.-Soviet relationship was summed up in a pledge by President Nixon and Brezhnev at their summit meeting in Washington in June 1973. Both countries agreed to "refrain from the threat or use of force

---

[4] Inter-continental and submarine-launched ballistic missiles.
[5] James E. Dornan, "Kissinger's Foreign Policy: Grand Design or Grand Delusion?" *Washington Report*, December 1975, p. 5. *Washington Report* is published by the American Security Council, Culpeper, Va. Dornan, chairman of the department of politics at Catholic University, Washington, D.C., served as a special assistant to House Minority Leader John J. Rhodes (R Ariz.), 1969-1974.

against the other party, against allies of the other party and against other countries, in circumstances which may endanger international peace and security." At the Helsinki Conference in the summer of 1975 the Soviet Union also agreed not to interfere "in the internal affairs of other countries."[6] Despite these agreements, the Soviets have repeatedly indicated that détente does not preclude the kind of action they have undertaken in Angola.

American officials have maintained that covert U.S. assistance was sent to Angola only after "massive" supplies of Soviet arms were shipped to the Popular Movement for the Liberation of Angola (MPLA). However, there is some question as to whether a decision by the so-called Forty Committee of the National Security Council[7] in January 1975 to funnel CIA money to the anti-Communist groups—the National Union for Total Independence of Angola (UNITA) and the National Front for the Liberation of Angola (FNLA)—did not precipitate Russian action. U.S. assistance was undertaken and must continue, Ford and Kissinger contend, not because the United States has any direct national interest in Angola but because it is vitally important to this country's position in the world to prevent a Soviet takeover there.

Opponents of the administration's Angolan policy call it shortsighted. They reason that it puts the United States into alliance with white-ruled South Africa, gives American support to the weaker and losing side in the conflict, creates the danger of involving this country in another Vietnam, and fails to recognize Soviet ties to the MLPA may dissolve quickly even if it wins. Russian intervention in Africa is reported to be resented there.[8]

To those critics who maintain that the United States has learned nothing from its Vietnam experience, President Ford's statement after the Senate voted to cut off aid to Angola was illustrative. The vote, he said, could deprive "us of our ability to help the people of Angola...decide their own fate." He added that "we have over a period of time helped to maintain free governments." Observers were quick to point out that

---

[6] The Conference on Security and Cooperation in Europe, held July 30-Aug. 1, 1975, was attended by 33 European nations, the United States and Canada. The parties signed a nonbinding agreement which called for a greater exchange of people, ideas and information, and recognition of existing borders in Europe.

[7] The Forty Committee derives its name from the 1969 National Security Council Memorandum No. 40 and has responsibility for approving all secret CIA operations. The committee consists of the Assistant to the President for National Security Affairs, Brent Scowcroft; Under Secretary of State, Joseph J. Sisco; Deputy Secretary of Defense, William P. Clements; chairman of the Joint Chiefs of Staff, Gen. George S. Brown; and Director of the CIA, George Bush.

[8] African suspicion of the Soviet Union was evident at the Organization of African Unity meeting in Addis Ababa, Ethiopia, Jan. 10-13, 1976. Many observers had expected the majority of African nations to recognize the Soviet-backed MLPA as a legitimate authority in Angola. However, 22 voted in favor of recognition and 22 others voted to recognize no faction.

Washington's current pursuit of global stability often makes it difficult for the United States to support democratic change in other countries.

This country now backs regimes in South Korea, the Philippines, Brazil and Chile which hardly qualify as bastions of democracy. The Nixon administration supported the colonels who had overthrown the duly elected government in Greece in 1967. Their ouster in 1974 was followed by a wave of anti-Americanism in that country.[9] The United States has acknowledged CIA involvement in the overthrow of President Salvador Allende Gossens of Chile in 1973. Allende, a Marxist, had been voted into office in a free national election three years earlier.

Comparison of U.S.-Russian Military Spending

At the heart of the criticisms of Kissinger's grand strategy is skepticism about his ability to preserve a Metternichian status quo[10] and concern over his alleged inattention to changes in the military balance between the U.S. and Russia. Faced with reports of a spectacular rise in Soviet defense capabilities in the past decade, the foes of détente are calling for higher U.S. defense spending. President Ford took this concern into consideration in presenting his budget message to Congress in January. In it, he asked Congress to approve $100.1 billion for defense in fiscal 1977, almost $9 billion more than was being spent in fiscal 1976.

Schlesinger has warned of Soviet military gains at American expense. He said on "Meet the Press" (NBC-TV) Nov. 23: "We as a nation are indulging in an ostrich syndrome in burying our heads in the sand.... The Soviets have increased their military establishment to over four million men. Today, they have twice as many men as we have. They have, in recent years, produced four times as many subs and surface combatants as we have. They are producing 70 per cent more tactical aircraft. In ground equipment, it is a production ratio of seven and eight to one.... They are outspending us, leaving pensions aside, by some 45 per cent and the trend is worsening."

Acknowledging the difficulties involved in comparing Soviet and American defense expenditures, the London-based International Institute for Strategic Studies reported in its survey of

---

[9] Anti-Americanism in Greece was worsened by the Ford administration's opposition to Congress' cutoff of military aid to Turkey after the Turkish invasion of Cyprus in 1974. Kissinger maintained that Turkey's strategic position on the Soviet border made it essential that the United States not alienate the Turks.

[10] Metternich, the 19th century Austrian statesman, was instrumental in creating a European balance of power opposed to revolutionary change. Kissinger, in his book *A World Restored* (1957), was lavish in his praise for the conservative Austrian's ability to ensure peace for almost a century in Europe after the Congress of Vienna in 1815.

"The Military Balance, 1975-1976" that Russia was outspending the United States by more than $10 billion a year *(see box, p. 55).* Barry M. Blechman of the Brookings Institution wrote recently that U.S. defense expenditures exceeded those of the Soviet Union by almost 20 per cent in 1964 but "are now only 70 per cent of the Soviet total." He said that in strategic nuclear weapons the U.S. lead of 7 to 1 in 1965 had changed to a Soviet edge of 1.3 to 1 by 1975. The Russians have also markedly improved the quality and quantity of their forces in Europe and their naval fleet, he added.[11]

What most concerns many American strategists is not that the military balance may have changed in favor of the Russians but that if current trends continue both the military and political positions of the United States will deteriorate. They say a decline in strength has already brought into question America's willingness or ability to defend the more than 40 nations with whom it has collective or bilateral security treaties.

Issues of Isolation and Involvement

I NTERNATIONALISTS like Kissinger, aware of recent disillusionment with America's involvement in the world, have expressed concern that the United States may be retreating into isolationism. Throughout American history, the opposing trends of isolation and intervention have alternately dominated foreign policy. For its first century the new nation managed, with few exceptions, to remain aloof from international squabbles.

Three factors—the country's physical isolation, the British Navy's control of the seas and an effectively maintained balance of power in Europe—enabled the United States to pursue a non-interventionist foreign policy in its formative years. Early American presidents insisted that the country avoid involvement in conflicts beyond its borders. After the outbreak of fighting between Britain and France, President Washington issued a Proclamation of Neutrality in 1793. Three years later, in his farewell address to the nation, Washington called for a policy of "no entangling alliances."

President Monroe repeated Washington's dictum in his annual message to Congress on Dec. 2, 1823. He recommended that the nation abstain from the "wars of the European powers in matters relating to themselves." Nevertheless, there was an in-

---

[11] Handicapping the Arms Race." *The New Republic,* Jan. 3&10, 1976, pp. 19-21.

U.S.-Soviet Defense Spending

(in billions of dollars)

	1972	1973	1974	1975
United States	77.6	78.4	84.3	92.8*
Soviet Union	84.4	88.9	96.4	103.8*

* Expected outlay in fiscal year 1976
SOURCE: The International Institute for Strategic Studies

terventionist aspect to Monroe's address, later known as the Monroe Doctrine. In it, he declared that the United States would consider any attempt by the European powers "to extend their system to any portion of this hemisphere as dangerous to our peace and security."

It was not until the end of the last century that the Monroe Doctrine was used to justify American intervention in Latin America. By then, the American West had been won and Manifest Destiny turned outward. The United States went to war with Spain in 1898 over Cuba and emerged from the conflict with overseas outposts as distant as the Philippines. The war was the forerunner of many interventions in Latin America in the next three decades.

In response to a British, German and Italian blockade of Venezuelan ports in 1902, President Theodore Roosevelt set forth his corollary to the Monroe Doctrine in his annual message to Congress on Dec. 6, 1904: "Chronic wrongdoing, or an impotence which results in a general loosening of the ties of civilized society, may in America as elsewhere ultimately require intervention by some civilized nation, and in the western hemisphere the adherence of the United States to the Monroe Doctrine may force the United States in flagrant cases of such wrongdoing or impotence to the exercise of an international police power." The first action under the corollary was intervention in the Dominican Republic in 1905 to collect debts owed the United States.

America became involved directly in a European conflict for the first time in World War I. The country entered the war under President Wilson's idealistic slogan of making the world "safe for democracy." After the Allied victory, Americans soon showed that they had little taste for active involvement in the world. The Senate, on March 19, 1920, rejected the Treaty of Versailles which embodied peace terms with Germany and the

Wilson-inspired Covenant of the League of Nations. The Senate's rejection of the treaty marked a return to isolationism for the next two decades.[12]

Role as World's Policeman After World War II

World War II forced the United States out of its isolationism and into a postwar role of world leadership. The country assumed its new role not by choice but by necessity; there was no other nation to fill the global power vacuum. For a brief time after the war ended in 1945, it seemed as if Wilson's dream of world peace and harmony had become a reality. The German, Italian and Japanese dictatorships had been defeated and the United Nations Charter was a rallying call for freedom and democracy.

The hope and harmony that characterized the immediate postwar period did not last long. Within two years, the Cold War was under way and the United States committed itself to a policy of containing Soviet communism. President Truman, in an address to Congress on March 12, 1947, pledged American support for "free people who are resisting attempted subjugation." The Truman Doctrine was first applied with military and economic aid to Greece and Turkey, both threatened by Communist pressures.

Containment during the Cold War resulted in a global network of regional and binational security pacts designed to prevent Communist expansion or subversion.[13] The military side of the containment policy was deterrence. Deterrence was based on the assumption that the Soviet Union was America's enemy and that survival depended on a strong defense. This meant that the United States not only needed tactical and nuclear forces capable of deterring Russian aggression but had to convince the Russians that, if provoked, it was determined to use them.

There were two aspects to America's global strategy during the Cold War. One was a commitment to defend nations or peoples striving to be free from communism. This aspect of containment was summed up by President Kennedy in his inaugural address in January 1961: "Let every nation know, whether it wishes us well or ill, that we shall pay any price, bear any burden, meet any hardship, support any friend, oppose any foe to assure the survival and the success of liberty."

---

[12] The provision for the League of Nations was contained in Section I of the Treaty of Versailles. The Senate accepted peace terms with Germany, but not U.S. adherence to the League, in 1921.

[13] These included the Inter-American Treaty of Reciprocal Assistance, set up by western hemispheric nations in 1947; the North Atlantic Treaty Organization (NATO), organized by the U.S., Canada and 10 Western European countries in 1949; and the Southeast Asia Treaty Organization (SEATO), established by Australia, France, Britain, New Zealand, Pakistan, the Philippines, Thailand and the U.S. in 1954. By the early 1970s, the United States was committed in some form or other to the security of more than 70 nations.

The other side of containment, and increasingly the predominant one, showed little concern for freedom and great willingness to support repressive regimes as long as they were unequivocally anti-Communist. According to Arthur M. Schlesinger Jr., Kennedy said at the time of dictator Rafael Trujillo's assassination in the Dominican Republic in 1961 that there were "three possibilities in descending order of preference: a democratic regime, a continuation of the Trujillo regime, or a Castro regime. We ought to aim at the first, but we really can't renounce the second until we are sure that we can avoid the third."[14]

Containment Policy and Involvement in Vietnam

From Korea to Lebanon to the Caribbean and finally to Southeast Asia, the United States actively pursued a policy of containing communism. Policymakers in Washington acted on the assumption that Communist expansion anywhere directly endangered the nation's security. Shortly after the North Korean army invaded South Korea in June 1950, President Truman "decided to meet force with force, extending the European containment concept to Asia."[15]

President Eisenhower ordered the U.S. Marines into Lebanon in July 1958, citing the 1957 Eisenhower Doctrine which gave the President authority to use the armed forces to assist any nation in the Middle East threatened by aggression from a Communist-dominated country. Eisenhower insisted that sending the Marines to Lebanon was "essential to the welfare of the United states" *(see box, p. 59)*.

Eisenhower also approved a CIA operation in Guatemala which resulted in the overthrow of leftist President Jacobo Arbenz Guzman in 1954. As Fidel Castro moved closer toward Soviet communism, the agency proposed to Eisenhower that an armed force of Cuban exiles be organized in Guatemala to invade Cuba. This project was approved by Eisenhower's successor, John F. Kennedy, and insurgents were landed at the Bay of Pigs on April 17, 1961. The invasion was a spectacular failure; within a few days Castro's forces had killed or captured almost all of the invaders.

It is now often said that American actions to contain communism after World War II made U.S. involvement in Vietnam inevitable. The United States began sending economic and military aid to the French in Indochina in May 1950, a year after China fell to the Communists and four years before the French were defeated at Dienbienphu. As the North Vietnamese under Ho Chi Minh continued to gather strength during the early

---

[14] Arthur M. Schlesinger Jr., *A Thousand Days* (1965), p. 704.
[15] Sheldon W. Simon, *Asian Neutralism and U.S. Policy* (1975), p. 3.

1960s, Washington sent military advisory personnel and more aid to Saigon. In March 1965, American ground troops joined the battle.[16]

In defense of intervention, official Washington invoked the domino theory[17] and reiterated the concept of self-determination for foreign peoples. President Johnson spoke of "the right of each people to govern themselves and to shape their own institutions" in his 1966 State of the Union message. "A peaceful world order will be possible only when each country walks the way it has chosen to walk," he said. "We follow this principle abroad...by continued hostility to the rule of the many by the few."

By the late 1960s, anti-war sentiment had reached a peak and Congress responded by retreating from its earlier support of the war. One of the original cold warriors, Richard M. Nixon, called for a new foreign policy soon after becoming President in 1969. Nixon and his national security adviser, Henry A. Kissinger, agreed that the country could not abandon its allies without losing credibility throughout the world. Nevertheless, the United States could no longer be counted upon to come automatically to the defense of all nations threatened by subversion or attack.[18]

The President soon outlined the new policy known as the Nixon Doctrine.[19] "We will help where it makes a real difference and is considered in our interest." But the U.S. "cannot—and will not—conceive *all* the plans, design *all* the programs, execute *all* the decisions and undertake *all* the defense of the free nations of the world [his emphasis]." The Nixon Doctrine seemed to imply that America's role as global policeman had come to an end; the country would henceforth intervene only where its national security was directly threatened.

Demands for Change After Debacle in Indochina

Vietnam, it has been said, marked the end of an era. Under the Nixon Doctrine, the national self-interest, not rigid anticommunism or a desire to make the world "safe for democracy," would govern American foreign policy. "One lesson we must surely learn from Vietnam is that new commitments to our national honor and prestige must be carefully weighed," Kissinger has said. "We must weigh carefully—as we failed to

---

[16] For background on American intervention and withdrawal, see "Vietnam Aftermath," *E.R.R.*, 1974 Vol. I, pp. 43-60.

[17] The domino theory, first enunciated by Dwight D. Eisenhower in 1950, held that without American support, all nations in a particular area would fall—one by one—like dominoes to the Communists.

[18] See "Foreign Policy Making," *E.R.R.*, 1975 Vol. I, p. 43, and "Peacetime Defense Spending," *E.R.R.*, 1974 Vol. I, p. 261.

[19] The Nixon Doctrine was first enunciated at a presidential press conference on the island of Guam, July 25, 1969, during Nixon's trip to eight countries in Asia and Europe. It was included in "United States Foreign Policy for the 1970s," President Nixon's report to Congress on Feb. 18, 1970.

Lebanon and the Lowered American Profile

Lebanon is often cited as an example of the change in U.S. global policy in the past two decades. In 1958, Lebanese President Camille Chamoun asked the United States to send troops to protect the country's independence against what was characterized as a Communist-inspired insurrection by Arab nationalists. In response, President Eisenhower dispatched 10,000 U.S. Marines to the country in July. They left in October.

Today the country is beset by bloody civil strife that has pitted leftist Moslems and Palestinians against conservative Christians. Chamon, now the Interior Minister, asked early this year for U.S. assistance to protect the integrity of the Christian-dominated, pro-western government. Although the Moslems and Palestinians have close ties with the pro-Soviet-Arab government in Syria, the United States refused to intervene.

do in the early sixties—the long-term consequences of new engagements. We must not overextend ourselves, promising what is not either in our interest or within our capability."[20]

The new global strategy entailed a shift from containment to détente. Détente was "a more realistic method than containment for preserving...the status quo generally favorable to American patronage."[21] Nixon said that détente, combined with a strong defense, was "a way to create vested interests on both sides in restraint and the strengthening of peace." Détente and the Nixon Doctrine can also be seen as a way of counteracting the post-Vietnam spirit of isolationism and disillusionment with America's global role. In a nationwide poll conducted in late 1972, public opinion analysts William Watts and Lloyd A. Free said that 73 per cent of the people they questioned agreed with the statement: "We shouldn't think so much in international terms but concentrate more on national problems here at home." Only 55 per cent had agreed in 1964.

It can be argued that the Nixon Doctrine brought about a significant change in American global strategy. It can also be argued that containment still remains the basic ingredient in U.S. foreign policy. Washington has tended to practice restraint in such areas as the Middle East where U.S.-Soviet interests are directly involved. But when the likelihood of a direct confrontation appears minimal, the United States is apt to take strong action if unfriendly forces threaten to take power. Only once in the post-Vietnam era has the United States undertaken direct

---

[20] Quoted in *The Defense Monitor,* September 1975, p. 2. The *Monitor* is published by the Center for Defense Information in Washington, D.C., a non-governmental group.

[21] J. L. S. Girling, " 'Kissingerism': The Enduring Problems," *International Affairs,* July 1975, pp. 325-326. Girling is a fellow in international relations at the Australian National University.

military action. In May 1975, the new Communist government in Cambodia seized the U.S. merchant ship Mayaguez. President Ford immediately dispatched marines and airpower to the scene to rescue the vessel.

Limited militarily by public and congressional demands for "no more Vietnams," Washington has relied on covert activities to ensure the stability of friendly governments or to topple hostile regimes. Although such activities apparently have been going on for decades, recent disclosures[22] of covert CIA operations in Cuba, Chile, Portugal, Italy, and Angola have brought into question the agency's ability to function effectively when leaks threaten to undermine its undertakings. Disclosures of assassination plots against foreign leaders[23] and large subsidies to parties or groups deemed friendly to the United States have spurred Congress to demand that certain activities be curtailed and that Congress be given some control over agency operations. In an amendment to the Foreign Assistance Act of 1974, Congress stipulated that no money could be spent by or for the CIA "unless or until the President finds that each such operation is important to the national security" and notifies the congressional committees involved.

In his 1976 State of the Union address on Jan. 19, President Ford maintained that undermining of American intelligence operations increases rather than decreases the danger of direct American involvement in armed conflict. "Our adversaries are encouraged to attempt new adventures, while our own ability to monitor events, and to influence events short of military action, is undermined," he said.

Global Policy in Age of Transition

CONGRESS'S REASSERTION of its role in foreign policy has not been limited to countering specific administration-backed policies in Southeast Asia, Turkey and Angola or CIA freedom from legislative oversight. The Senate Foreign Relations Committee is conducting a study of U.S. global strategy for the decade ahead. The study was characterized by

---

[22] By, among others, the House Select Committee on Intelligence, headed by Rep. Otis G. Pike (D N.Y.), the Senate Select Committee on Intelligence, headed by Sen. Frank Church (D Idaho), former CIA employees and investigative news reporters.

[23] According to the Senate Intelligence Committee, the CIA engaged in plots to murder Fidel Castro between 1960 and 1965 and to assassinate Congolese Premier Patrice Lumumba in the 1960s. The committee also said it had found that American officials encouraged or were privy to plots which resulted in the deaths of Rafael Trujillo in the Dominican Republic in 1961, Ngo Dinh Diem of South Vietnam in 1963 and Gen. Rene Schneider of Chile in 1970.

the committee chairman, Sen. John J. Sparkman (D Ala.), as "most appropriate as the country enters its third century and passes from the post-World War II and Vietnam eras looking for new ideas."

Richard J. Barnet calls for a "great foreign policy debate," a broad questioning of the "basic assumptions" of U.S. global strategy. The discussion of current American policy, he asserts, "accepts uncritically the Cold War model of reality." Détente notwithstanding, American leaders still cling to the propositions that "Soviet power must be contained by maintaining superior nuclear forces and projecting conventional military might through alliances, military aid arrangements and foreign bases."[24] Critics of current American foreign policy assert that this bicentennial year would be an appropriate time to reassess U.S. global strategy. They say that the country founded 200 years ago in revolution has become the backer of stability and the status quo, the ally of repressive right-wing dictatorships and the enemy of economic and social reform.

Charge That U.S. Seeks to Maintain Status Quo

Those opposed to what Hans Morgenthau calls the American commitment to "an inviable status quo" question the ability of the United States to preserve a stable world order in an unstable world. The number of representative democracies has dwindled to less than 25; the governments of the 142 countries represented in the United Nations are overthrown on an average of once every 11 years.[25] It is argued that the U.S. quest for global stability has allowed the Soviet Union to take the offensive and to demonstrate to the world its support for the struggle for national liberation.

To many observers, the United States has failed to take into account the fiercely nationalistic quality that marks most struggles for independence in the developing world. The same criticism is made about U.S. opposition to national Communist parties in western Europe. The Italian Communist Party, which has about 1.7 million members and received a third of the vote in local elections in June 1975, has long proclaimed its independence from Moscow and its dedication to democratic government, freedom of speech and press, and a multi-party system.[26] Italian Communist leader Enrico Berlinguer has gone so far as to assert that if, as many expect, his party wins a majority in future national elections, it would support continued Italian membership in NATO and the European Economic Com-

[24] "The Great Foreign Policy Debate We Ought to Be Having," *The New Republic,* Jan. 17, 1976, p. 17. Barnet is co-director of the Institute for Policy Studies in Washington, D.C.

[25] According to Daniel Patrick Moynihan, then U.S. ambassador to the U.N., in a speech to the AFL-CIO annual convention in San Francisco, Oct. 3, 1975.

[26] See "Italy's Threatened Democracy," *E.R.R.,* 1975 Vol. I, pp. 14-19.

munity (EEC). Kissinger has questioned Communist pledges to work within the democratic framework. At the same time, he has been reported to have predicted that all Europe would be Marxist-dominated within 10 years.

Question of Economic Policies and Arms Sales

The same quest for stability that governs America's global politics also influences its world economic policies. Kissinger encourages U.S. trade with the Soviet Union as a means of strengthening détente but takes a hard line toward Third-World countries that attempt to alter the economic status quo.[27] At the Conference on International Economic Cooperation in Paris in December 1975,[28] Kissinger warned developing countries that they should not expect help from the United States if they continued to support efforts by the Organization of Petroleum Exporting Countries to keep prices high. *The New York Times* reported Jan. 9, 1976, it had been told by a State Department official that Kissinger was implementing a policy of denying aid to countries that sided against the United States.

The interests of "have" and "have not" nations also conflict in regard to U.S. policy toward nuclear weapons and arms sales. The United States has opposed efforts by non-nuclear nations to add a protocol to the Nuclear Non-Proliferation Treaty of 1968 committing the nuclear powers to refrain from threatening or using atomic weapons against non-nuclear countries. U.S. opposition is based on the belief that the protocol would weaken security commitments between this country and its allies.[29] In the absence of such a commitment, it is argued, other nations will feel impelled to join the nuclear club, now consisting of the United States, the Soviet Union, Britain, France, China and India.[30] According to Department of Defense estimates, the U.S. government will sell $9.8 billion worth of arms to other countries in fiscal year 1976. Commercial sales abroad are expected to exceed $2 billion.

At a time when détente is being denounced by the political right as a sell-out to the Soviet Union and by the political left as insensitive toward the rest of the world, there is one foreign policy priority that elicits strong bipartisan support: a strengthening of the U.S. ties with Western Europe and Japan. While Kissinger has been accused of undermining U.S. relations with traditional allies, he has frequently called for U.S.-

---

[27] In a speech in Atlanta June 23, 1975,. Kissinger indicated that he saw no reason to overhaul the existing system. "The present global economic system is large enough to encompass the well-being of consumers and producers, rich and poor."

[28] Attended by 12 developing countries, seven oil-producing states and 16 industrial nations to set guidelines on energy, finance, development aid and raw materials.

[29] For background, see "Nuclear Safeguards," *E.R.R.*, 1974 Vol. II, pp. 867-884.

[30] For a discussion of these views, see the published proceedings of the Harvard-MIT Arms Control Seminar in *Harvard Magazine*, November 1975.

European-Japanese "solidarity" in facing global political and economic problems. Henry Owen, former policy planning director at the State Department and now with the Brookings Institution, has argued for years that closer relations between the United States, Western Europe and Japan "should be the main focus of U.S. policy."[31]

Agreeable as this suggestion might be, there are barriers to its fruition. American officials recall the European reluctance to allow the United States to use NATO bases to transport military equipment to Israel during the 1973 war in the Middle East and are aware of the European questioning of U.S. global aims.

Prof. Richard Rosecrance of Cornell, president of the International Studies Association, considers the old alliances to be disintegrating and potentially dangerous. "As nuclear weapons spread and the economic disruption of industrial economies proceeds, nothing short of a partial Soviet-American entente will provide the necessary structure in which present destabilizing currents can be contained." Such an arrangement, Rosecrance maintains, would not be a means of ensuring superpower global hegemony nor would it rule out "closer Sino-American relations" and the continuation of NATO or the Warsaw Pact. What it would help to prevent is the forging of "ties with one nation or group at the expense of another" and the creation of a "new polarization in world politics."[32]

A U.S.-Soviet or U.S.-European-Japanese entente is often recommended as a preferable alternative to global anarchy. But there are those who consider these options unrealistic. The power and influence that the United States and Russia commanded only a few years ago have lessened considerably, they assert, and alliance systems have become more fragile in an increasingly multipolar world. In their view, it would be wiser for the United States to follow a more pragmatic and flexible balance-of-power policy. Russia's split with China might be furthered by more cooperation between Washington and Peking. It is pointed out that after the U.S. reconciliation with China in 1972, the Soviet Union became more receptive to the signing of agreements with the United States to limit strategic weapons and to encourage peaceful competition.

These and other choices lie ahead. While there is as yet no consensus on what American foreign policy should be, there is widespread agreement that the United States, chastened by the lessons of Vietnam, beset by economic problems at home and confronted with growing Soviet power, needs to reevaluate its present global strategy.

[31] Henry Owen (ed.), *The Next Phase in Foreign Policy* (1973), p. 330.
[32] "Détente or Entente," *Foreign Affairs*, April 1975, p. 481.

Selected Bibliography

Books

Bloomfield, Lincoln P. and Irirangi C., *The U.S., Interdependence and World Order*, Foreign Policy Association, 1975.

Brown, Seyom, *New Forces in World Politics*, The Brookings Institution, 1974.

Diebold, William, *The United States and the Industrial World: American Foreign Economic Policy in the 1970s*, Praeger, 1972.

Kalb, Marvin and Bernard, *Kissinger*, Little Brown, 1974.

Kissinger, Henry A., *The Necessity for Choice*, Harper & Row, 1961.

—*Nuclear Weapons and Foreign Policy*, Harper & Row, 1957.

—*A World Restored*, Houghton Mifflin, 1957.

Lake, Anthony (ed.), *Legacy of Vietnam*, New York University Press, 1975.

Owen, Henry (ed.), *The Next Phase in Foreign Policy*, The Brookings Institution, 1973.

Petrov, Vladimir, *U.S.-Soviet Detente: Past and Future*, American Enterprise Institute for Public Policy Research, 1975.

Simon, Sheldon W., *Asian Neutralism and U.S. Policy*, American Enterprise Institute for Public Policy Research, 1975.

Articles

Barnet, Richard J., "The Great Foreign Policy Debate We Ought to Be Having," *The New Republic*, Jan. 17, 1976.

Blechman, Barry M., "Handicapping the Arms Race," *The New Republic*, Jan. 3 & 10, 1976.

The Defense Monitor, selected issues.

Dornan, James E., "Kissinger's Foreign Policy: Grand Design or Grand Delusion?" *Washington Report*, December 1975.

Feld, Bernard T., "What's Wrong With SALT?" *Arms Control Today*, December 1975.

Foreign Affairs, selected issues.

Foreign Policy, selected issues.

Girling, J. L. S., " 'Kissingerism': The Enduring Problems," *International Affairs*, July 1975.

Morgenthau, Hans J., "Three Paradoxes," *The New Republic*, Oct. 11, 1975.

"Nuclear War by 1999?" *Harvard Magazine*, November 1975.

Sonnenfeldt, Helmut, "The Meaning of Detente," *Naval War College Review*, July-August 1975.

Reports and Studies

The Brookings Institution, selected studies.

Democratic Study Group, selected fact sheets.

Editorial Research Reports: "Foreign Policy Making," 1975 Vol. I, p. 43; "Nuclear Safeguards," 1974 Vol. II, p. 867; "Peacetime Defense Spending," 1974 Vol. I, p. 263; "Trends in U.S.-Soviet Relations," 1973 Vol. I, p. 300; "Vietnam Aftermath," 1974 Vol. I, p. 43.

International Institute for Strategic Studies, "The Military Balance, 1975-76," 1975.

Rural Migration

by

David Boorstin

**Aug. 15
1 9 7 5**

RURAL MIGRATION

A RETIRED COUPLE returns to the small town they left during the Depression. A young couple decides to raise their children outside the city. A manufacturer chooses to build his company's new plant in a rural industrial park. A farmer's daughter stays home and attends the local college. All of these actions form part of a new and largely unforeseen trend in American life. In the words of demographer Calvin L. Beale: "The vast rural-to-urban migration of people that was the common pattern of U.S. population movement in the decades after World War II has been halted and, on balance, even reversed. In the eyes of many Americans, the appeal of major urban areas has diminished and the attractiveness of rural and small town communities has increased, economically and otherwise."[1]

For the first time in this century, and perhaps in the history of the United States, the population in metropolitan areas *(see box, p. 71)* is growing more slowly than elsewhere. This reversal of a longtime trend is all the more pronounced because urban migration remained strong through the 1960s. During that decade, metropolitan counties grew almost twice as fast as other counties. Census Bureau estimates for the first three years of this decade[2] portrayed the turnabout: metropolitan areas grew only 2.9 per cent while nonmetropolitan areas gained 4.2 per cent. Other Census Bureau estimates indicate that except for natural growth—more births than deaths—the metropolitan areas actually would have lost population. From March 1970 to March 1974, almost six million people moved out while only slightly more than four million moved in.[3]

America is not about to become a rural society; about three-quarters of its 211 million people now live in cities and

---

[1] "The Revival of Population Growth in Nonmetropolitan America," report based on a paper presented at the Conference on Population Distribution, Belmont, Md., Jan. 29-31, 1975, p. 1. Beale, an expert on rural population, is the leader of the Population Studies Group of the Department of Agriculture's Economic Research Service.

[2] From April 1970, when the last decennial census was taken, until July 1973, when the last complete set of county estimates was released. The 1974 figures are not yet available for all states.

[3] Children of ages four or younger were not counted because they had been born during that time. Their inclusion would have distorted the statistics.

hundreds of thousands will continue to move to cities each year. Metropolitan life will continue to dominate the United States for the foreseeable future, as it does every modern nation. To some extent the new figures still reflect this country's urban orientation. They show that about five-eighths of the gain in non-metropolitan population occurred in counties adjacent to metropolitan areas. This growth could be seen as a continuation of urban and suburban sprawl. But remote rural counties have also been growing more rapidly than metropolitan counties. Thus it appears that there has been a significant shift toward rural America, both to the open country and the small town. The causes of this shift are evidence of profound changes in American life, and the effects on American culture and public policy may be no less deep.

Social Causes of Population Shift to the Land

Some see the new migration as the result of a critical transition in American life. They argue that American society has left its growth phase and is heading for equilibrium of some sort. Professor Jay W. Forrester of the Massachusetts Institute of Technology, who has attracted attention and controversy for his views on world and urban dynamics, says: "In the life cycle of the economic growth of a country I believe you'll find that generally speaking people will move from the country to the city in the growth phase and back to the country in the equilibrium phase."[4]

On a personal level, however, the increased likelihood that city dwellers will move to the country, or that country people will stay where they are, reflects change in individual attitudes. There are twin considerations—escaping what is unpleasant and looking for something better. Americans came to the cities in the first place because they felt that cities offered superior living conditions and economic opportunities. But for many people, the cities now offer a catalogue of social ills. Crime and drugs, pollution, congestion, decay, racial tension and financial crises have already pushed millions out of the cities and into the suburbs.

But city problems spread outward with the population. At the same time, according to sociologists and public-opinion surveys, many Americans began to feel a growing sense of powerlessness and loss of control over their lives in a highly organized society. It is not surprising that in this social climate the countryside came to appear a place of refuge. Television and advertising caught this mood and magnified it. In a generation, the image of rural life changed from that of *Tobacco Road* to that of *The Waltons.*

---

[4] Interviewed by Haynes Johnson in *The Washington Post*, June 8, 1975.

Four Rapidly Growing Nonmetropolitan Regions

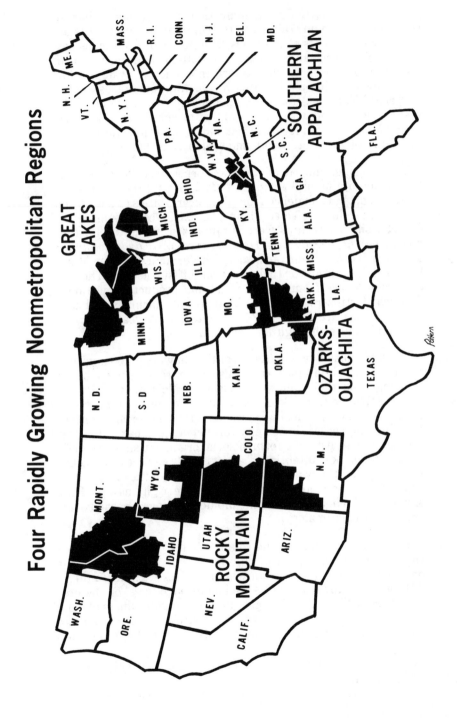

GREAT LAKES

SOUTHERN APPALACHIAN

OZARKS-OUACHITA

ROCKY MOUNTAIN

WASH.
ORE.
CALIF.
NEV.
IDAHO
MONT.
WYO.
UTAH
ARIZ.
COLO.
N. M.
N. D.
S. D.
NEB.
KAN.
OKLA.
TEXAS
MINN.
IOWA
MO.
ARK.
LA.
WIS.
ILL.
MICH.
IND.
OHIO
KY.
TENN.
MISS.
ALA.
GA.
FLA.
S. C.
N. C.
VA.
W. VA.
PA.
N. Y.
VT.
N. H.
ME.
MASS.
R. I.
CONN.
N. J.
DEL.
MD.

At its extreme, the rural migration has become a "back to the land" movement, related to the communal experiments and anti-war sentiments of the 1960s. Thousands of Americans have gone back to the land in search of self-sufficiency, in an antagonistic response to the American economic system which they view as being obsessed with consumption, status and the "rat race." The back-to-the-land people seek security outside the cash economy, and with a minimum of mechanical and technical help. "Make do with less" is their motto, and the guiding lights for many of them are Scott and Helen Nearing.

The Nearings moved from New York City to a farm in the Green Mountains of Vermont in 1932, during the Depression. They sought independence from the uncertainties of a capitalist society that had rejected their pacifism, vegetarianism and collectivism. Their aims were summarized in the title of their book, *Living the Good Life: How to Live Sanely and Simply in a Troubled World.*[5] Their farms, first in Vermont and then Maine, became laboratories for their ideas on self-sufficiency. These include abstinence from meat and animal products, rejection of chemical fertilizers, and the barest use of machines and cash. The Nearings are hosts to 2,500 visitors each year and reach thousands more through lectures and books.

Most of those who choose rural life, however, do so without the clearcut philosophy and sense of purpose shown by the Nearings and their followers. Susan S. McDonald, writing in *National Review,* mocked the attitude of one set of "young pioneers" who "are losing patience with the urban frontier." "Having stopped off in the city for a strategic year or two, and found it to be a perverse form of social organization which defies good will and best intentions," she wrote, "they are now packing their Volvo station wagons and spinning out of the metropolitan orbit.... The only lofty living alternative right now is Rural America, which, at least for the moment, enjoys a paradoxically chaste yet chic image."[6]

For others, moving to the country is less a matter of choice than desperation. "Suburban life for us was a little like sitting on a bomb," explained a man who now lives with his family in Ashton, Ill., a town of 1,112. "We just decided to get out before a real tragedy hit."[7] The slow pace and the neighborliness of small communities, once thought of as a sources of social claustrophobia and rigidity, have proved satisfying to these migrants.

---

[5] Published in 1954 and reissued in 1972, the book has sold 111,000 copies in cloth and paperback.

[6] Susan S. McDonald, "Flight Patterns," *National Review,* May 9, 1975, p. 513.

[7] Quoted by Dale Wittner, "Return To Rural America: Seeking A Simpler Life," *Today's Health,* April 1975, p. 31.

And while Census Bureau figures do not yet show the effect, there is no doubt that in recent months large numbers of Americans have left the cities in search of jobs. According to Gerald Cornez, director of development for Travelers Aid-International Social Service of America, the average case load of his organization's 80 offices nationwide has increased 25 to 30 per cent over last year.[8] Many of these migrants are moving from one urban or suburban area to another, but it appears that others are heading for the countryside. During the Depression Thirties, jobless city dwellers moved to farms to keep from starving. But today, with unemployment insurance available and the decline in the number of family farms, the prevalence and permanence of this type of migration is unclear.

The transition from urban or suburban to rural life has been eased considerably by technology, and those who do not vehemently reject all aspects of city life can maintain contact with it. The Nearings "crossed a wide chasm" when they moved from downtown New York to Vermont: "We were leaping from the economic and social sophistication of a metropolis to a neighborhood in which few of the adults and none of the youngsters had ever visited a large city, in which every house was heated with wood and lighted with kerosene, and in which there was not a single flush toilet." They introduced local children to trains, coal, movies and even ice cream sodas.

Today's rural dwellers may enjoy a different life than their country cousins, but they share with them a new world of high-speed transportation and instant communication, and a national economy that has jumped from $56 billion in 1933 to more than $1.3 trillion. The Nearings left Vermont two decades

---

[8] The organization handled about 1.3 million pleas for assistance last year. Cornez was quoted in a *U.S. News & World Report* cover story, " 'Okies' of the '70s," March 24, 1975, p. 17.

ago because a large ski resort was built next to their farm. Now, in Harborside, Maine, they are troubled by the impending construction of at least one nearby nuclear power plant.

Rural Economic Development; Farming Decline

Developments such as those that have bothered the Nearings are in themselves both cause and effect of rural migration. In the 1960s, population decline was common in counties where more than one-third of the labor force was employed in any combination of agriculture, mining and railroad work at the beginning of the decade. This meant that by 1970, far fewer counties were primarily dependent on extractive industries. The decentralization trend in manufacturing during the 1960s brought new jobs to areas previously dependent on farming, mining or timber. More recently, service industries and trade rather than manufacturing have provided the impetus for rural economic growth. Manufacturing accounted for half of the job growth in non-metropolitan areas in 1962-69 but just 18 per cent in the following four years.[9]

The so-called "retirement counties" are the fastest growing of all, according to demographer Beale. They are defined as counties in which, during the 1960s, the number of incoming white residents of age 60 and older exceeded the outgoing by 15 per cent or more. The total population of these counties grew by an average of 25 per cent during that decade, and the pace has quickened since then.[10] Recreation and retirement activities have spread from the traditional areas in Florida and the Southwest to other regions. Clusters of retirement counties are found in the Upper Great Lakes (especially Michigan), the Ozarks, the hill country of central Texas, the Sierra Nevada foothills in California and the East Texas coastal plain.

More people are retiring earlier and with better pensions than in the past. Most federal workers, for example, are eligible to retire at age 55. Many retired persons flock to communities that already have attracted others in retirement. Moreover, these places also lure younger families, not only for their natural attractiveness or recreational facilities but for the jobs that develop around leisure communities.

Counties with senior state-supported colleges have shown a rate of growth well above the national average in recent years despite a nationwide slowdown in college enrollment growth. A local college increases the availability of higher education and makes the town more attractive for other development. Com-

---

[9] Beale, *op. cit.*, p. 9.
[10] The 1970-73 increase was estimated at 12.3 per cent.

munity colleges and technical schools frequently cooperate with businesses in providing training for new or expanded plants. A college or university also provides a cultural center for a rural area and lessens the gap between country and city.

The old picture of rural America is changing. Now only 400,-000 people, less than 1 per cent of the non-metropolitan population, live in heavily agricultural counties—counties with 40 per cent or more of their employment in farming. Economic and social changes have increased both rural population retention and immigration. And the new migrants themselves are likely to have a great impact on the areas to which they move. Those most prone to migration are in their twenties, and college graduates are more likely to move than those with less education.

Past American Migration Trends

E ACH OF THE FOUR great waves of transatlantic migration[11] which peopled the United States from 1844-1913 was essentially a rural exodus across national boundaries. These migrations were prompted by events such as the Irish potato famine in 1846 and the crisis of the 1880s in European agriculture brought about by competition with technologically advanced American farms. Most of these immigrants had been engaged in farming or unskilled labor, and one effect was that, as noted by the U.S. Immigration Commission in 1911, new mechanical devices and processes had to be invented to take ad-

[11] The four "boom" periods in migration from Europe were 1844-54; 1863-73; 1881-88 and 1903-13.

vantage of their labor by eliminating much of the skill and experience previously needed in many industrial occupations.[12]

Another effect was the westward expansion of the United States. When the first census was taken in 1790, not one American in twenty lived west of the Appalachian Mountains. Ninety years later, one-half of the country's inhabitants lived on land that had become a part of the United States since 1790. The 3.9 million Americans recorded in that first census were equally divided between the North (today's Northeast) and South, and those two regions grew at an even pace for much of the nation's history. But the expansion beyond the Appalachians filled the North Central region[13] to the point where it overtook them in population by 1870.

The truly phenomenal growth took place in the West.[14] First appearing in the census of 1850, the region grew in population over the next half-century almost ten times faster than the country as a whole. The other major pull of internal migration over the past century has been northward from the rural South *(see p. 79)*. In addition, there has been a movement more recently toward Florida and the Gulf Coast.[15]

Countryside's Long Decline; Signs of Reversal

America's longest continuing migratory trend has been the movement of people from farms to cities. The rural exodus has been especially swift since 1940, a year that America began to gear up for war, creating hundreds of thousands of industrial jobs and ending the Depression. The movement away from the land continued through the war and the following decades. The number of people employed solely or primarily in farming dropped from 9.5 million in 1940 to 3.5 million in 1972. From 1940 to 1960 the farm population was halved *(see table, p. 75)*. Rural America lost population despite high birth rates.

Typically, young people left and the old stayed behind. A "natural decrease" in population took place as more people were of an age to die than to have children, an imbalance almost unknown in rural America before the mid-1950s. And as the population aged, young adults had less incentive to remain.

Much of the rural population that did not make the migration to the metropolitan areas went instead to the towns and small

---

[12] *Abstract of Reports of the Immigration Commission*, vol. i, doc. no. 747, p. 494, Washington, D.C., 1911-12.

[13] So designated by the Census Bureau, embracing the historic Northwest Territory and some adjacent states of today's Midwest. They are Illinois, Indiana, Iowa, Kansas, Michigan, Minnesota, Missouri, Nebraska, North Dakota, South Dakota and Wisconsin.

[14] Comprising Arizona, Colorado, California, Idaho, Montana, Nevada, New Mexico, Oregon, Utah, Washington and Wyoming. The region now includes Alaska and Hawaii.

[15] See "Mobility in American Life," *E.R.R.*, 1973 Vol. I, pp. 341-347, and "Population Profile of the United States," *E.R.R.*, 1967 Vol. II, pp. 808-812.

Declining U.S. Farm Population

Year	Farm population (in millions)	Per cent of total	Per cent of rural population
1920	31.9	30.1	62.0
1930	30.5	24.9	56.7
1940	30.5	23.2	53.4
1950	23.0	15.3	42.5
1960	15.6	8.7	28.9
1970	9.7	4.8	18.0
1971*	9.4	4.6	**
1972*	9.6	4.6	**
1973*	9.4	4.5	**

*Estimates
**Not available
SOURCE: U.S. Department of Agriculture, Economic Research Service

cities. By the middle of the 1950s, the Department of Agriculture had begun to promote rural development and urge communities to seek industry or other sources of employment. The emerging Interstate Highway System began to shorten travel time and permit a wider dispersal of the population. "But only here and there in that decade were there actual population reversals from loss to gain in nonmetro areas—the beginnings of revival in the Colorado slopes; the start of recreation and retirement in the Ozarks; oil-related development in south Louisiana; and the sprawling influence of Atlanta, Kansas City, or Minneapolis-St. Paul on accessible nonmetro counties."[16]

By the mid-1960s, a variety of influences began to stabilize rural population. So much of the excess rural labor force had been drained off that the peak of potential outmigration had passed. Rural counties acquired manufacturing, and although many of the plants paid low wages, they provided badly needed employment for both men and women and substantially increased rural family income.

Recreational and retirement activities flourished, and "second homes" sprang up for weekend and vacation living. Dam-building had created lakes in even the most arid parts of the country and was visibly encouraging rural development. In short, the nation's growing affluence began filtering through to the countryside. As a result, net outmigration was reduced from 5.5 million in the 1950s to 2.2 million in the 1960s. Of the 2,272

---

[16] Beale, *op. cit.*, p. 3.

non-metropolitan counties that experienced migratory losses in the 1950s, 1,946 showed lighter losses in the 1960s.[17]

Two rural areas served as harbingers of change in the 1960s, illustrating the potential for the rural turnaround once the traditional reliance on agriculture had been minimized. One area stretched in an oval shape from St. Louis to Dallas, encompassing the Ozarks, the lower Arkansas Valley, the Ouachita Mountains, and northeast Texas. The other was bounded by Memphis, Louisville, Atlanta and Birmingham. Both areas, although relatively poor, ceased to lose population.

The country's rural population has remained remarkably stationary, at about 54 million, in each census after 1940. The nation's net population growth from 1940 to 1970, a total of 71 million, took place in urban and suburban areas. But there has been a great deal of flux within the rural population. Many rural areas have come to be classified as urban because of their growth. Declines in population have continued in the Great Plains, western Corn Belt, southern Appalachian coal areas, and the old Cotton Belt of the southern coastal plain—especially those parts with large black populations *(see p. 79)*. Sizable population growth has occurred between metropolitan areas of the lower Great Lakes and the Northeast, in the Far West, the Florida Peninsula, and the textile areas of the Southern Piedmont.

Public Concern With Effects of Rural Exodus

Perhaps surprisingly, the rural-to-urban movement did not become a matter of great importance to Americans until the mid-1960s. James L. Sundquist of the Brookings Institution identifies the turning point in a single word: Watts. "After the Watts riots in Los Angeles in 1965, and those that followed in other major cities in the next three summers, the people of the cities saw their own problems in a harsh new light," he wrote. "For the first time, the declining rural areas that had pressed their pleas for help in the face of urban indifference—if not hostility—found allies in the cities. The population flow that had resulted from rural stagnation and decline might not, it turned out, have been the cities' boon. Cities and countryside alike might have been ill-served by the forces that had made for population concentration. In a newly discovered mutual interest, then, lay the basis for political coalition."[18]

---

[17] Calvin L. Beale, "Rural Development: Population and Settlement Prospects," *Journal of Soil and Water Conservation*, January-February 1974, p. 26.

[18] James L. Sundquist, *Dispersing Population: What America Can Learn From Europe* (1975), p. 3.

It was realized that the urban problems of racial tension, crime, poverty, congestion and social alienation, and the problem of rural decay, were in fact two sides of the same coin. In 1968, for the first time, both political parties committed themselves in their election-year platforms to a national policy of balanced growth, stemming the flow from countryside to city. In the same year the National Governors' Conference said that "population imbalance is at the core of nearly every major social problem facing our nation today" and urged the adoption of policies to bring about a more even distribution of population among the states. The National Association of Counties and the United States Conference of Mayors echoed the concern.

President Nixon, in his 1970 State of the Union Message, spoke of "the emptying out" of rural America and the problems of the "violent" cities. In 1971 he proposed that rural regions "can become a new magnet for people seeking the good life, so that we can begin to see a reversal of the decades-long migration trend from rural America to urban America—a trend which has too often acted to deplete the countryside and overburden the cities, to weaken the heart of America and to add to the fat which saps our strength."[19] Congress committed itself to "a sound balance between rural and urban America" in the Agricultural Act of 1970, which urged "the highest priority" for "the revitalization and development of rural areas."

Despite this widespread concern, Sundquist said in a recent book, "The country is no nearer to the definition of a policy now than it was in 1968 and 1970, when the declarations of principle were made. Indeed, it has not even established a process for the formulation of a policy."[20] Tax subsidies were proposed primarily as welfare measures to relieve distressed communities, but these also would have increased job availability and population retention in rural areas. In three successive Congresses—in 1967, 1969 and 1971—Sen. James B. Pearson (R Kan.) introduced a bill offering tax credits to rural industry. With each reintroduction the bill drew additional sponsors but it never won passage. In 1971, Sen. Abraham A. Ribicoff (D Conn.) upset Pearson's strategy by demanding equal treatment for the central cities. Recognizing that his plan would be defeated without urban support, Pearson agreed to the Ribicoff amendment. But that aroused the opposition of Chairman Russell B. Long (D La.) and other senior members of the Senate Finance Committee, who successfully opposed the Pearson-Ribicoff proposal as being too costly.

---

[19] Remarks at the dedication of a navigation system at Catoosa, Okla., June 5, 1971, in *Public Papers of the Presidents, 1971*, p. 717.

[20] Sundquist, *op. cit.*, p. 7.

Ironically, at the same time that incentives for rural growth were failing at the national political level, millions of Americans were voicing their preference for the rural life. Many surveys produced evidence that they disliked large cities and preferred less concentrated patterns of settlement, although the data were not conclusive.

Change In Popular Feeling for Country Life

A major study which was undertaken in 1971 for the Commission on Population Growth and the American Future[21] found, for instance, that more than half of the 1,700 adult respondents said they wanted to live in a rural or small-town setting, although few of them actually were living there, as is shown in the following table:

	Large urban center	Small urban center	Rural or small town
Preferred residence	13%	33%	53%
Actual residence	28	41	32

Dissatisfaction with community size seemed to increase as size itself increased. These findings confirmed those of other surveys: 48 per cent of the respondents to a Harris poll in 1970 said they would prefer to live in a city or suburb while 47 per cent favored either a small town away from a city, or a farm; a series of Gallup polls between 1966 and 1972 showed a shift in preference from cities to rural areas.[22]

Other surveys indicated that for most people, the ideal residence was a small town or rural area within 30 minutes of a city of at least 50,000 people. This finding suggested that the basic trend of metropolitan sprawl was not being altered. However, Calvin L. Beale has pointed out that a second finding modified those results. "By a very wide margin (65 to 35 per cent), the big city people who preferred a nearby rural or small town residence ranked a more remote rural or small town place as their second choice, and thus as preferable to the big city," he wrote.[23]

Beale also noted that in the survey conducted for the Commission on Population Growth and the American Future, three-eighths of the people who expressed a desire to move to a

---

[21] Survey by Opinion Research Corp., reported in *Aspects of Population Growth Policy* (1972), Vol. 6 of research reports prepared for U.S. Commission on Population Growth and the American Future, Appendix A, pp. 498-509, and analyzed by Sara Mills Mazie and Steve Rawlings in "Public Attitude Toward Population Distribution Issues," *Population, Distribution, and Policy*, Vol. 5 of same research reports, pp. 603-615.

[22] Polls cited by Sundquist, *op. cit.*, pp. 24-26.

[23] "The Revival of Population Growth in Nonmetropolitan Areas," *op. cit.*, p. 16.

different type of locality declared that they were "very likely" to make such a move "within the next few years." Projecting this statistic on a national scale indicates, he said, "a potential of about 14 million people of all ages moving from metro cities and suburbs to smaller places and rural areas."

Effects of New Population Shift

THE MOST notable reversal in migration shown by the 1970 census was in the South, which for at least a century had seen more people move out than move in. The census showed that during the previous decade native southerners had been less inclined to go elsewhere, and that those who had already left were returning in larger numbers than ever.[24] This new pattern of migration has continued into this decade. From 1970 through 1973 the South experienced the largest net immigration of any of the four census regions.

Contrary to popular belief, return migration to the South is not primarily a movement of older persons "going home" to retire; it is a movement in which parents in their late twenties are the most likely to participate. In terms of race, the rate at which blacks return to the South has risen in the past 15 years, but they are still less likely to return than southern-born whites. *Ebony* magazine reported in 1971: "Many blacks, returning South to avoid northern crime and pollution problems, are enthusiastic with praise about the area's progress. None, however, ignore its numerous drawbacks."[25] Not only has the rate of return quickened, but perhaps more important, the rate of departure has slowed.[26] The black migration to and from the South appears to be changing in much the same general way as white migration did earlier.

Promise and Problems of Rural Repopulation

When millions of Americans moved from the cities to the suburbs, urbanologist Lewis Mumford observed, they had to pay "the penalty of popularity."[27] They brought with them many of the very problems they sought to escape. The rural migration

---

[24] See "Trends in Return Migration to the South," paper by Larry H. Long and Kristin A. Hansen to be published in the November 1975 issue of *Demography*. Long and Hansen are demographers in the Census Bureau's Population Division.

[25] "It's Good to be Home Again," *Ebony*, August 1971, p. 70.

[26] See "The Social and Economic Status of the Black Population in the United States 1974," Census Bureau publication dated July 1975 (Special Studies Series P-23, No. 54), p. 1.

[27] Lewis Mumford in *The End of Innocence—A Suburban Reader* (1972), p. 5. The book is edited by Charles M. Harr.

carries the seeds of the same threat, although it is often not apparent immediately. A great influx of new settlers in the countryside can change the character of rural life and destroy its appeal.

Rural communities view the influx both as a promise and as a threat. Increased employment, a better tax base and greater local amenities could be one result. On the other hand, especially where local growth is recreation-based, some of the local people may not fare so well as before. Recreation businesses tend to be seasonal and generally create only low-skill and low-paid jobs. Niles M. Hansen noted in his book *The Future of Non-metropolitan America* (1973):

> Interviews with local and state officials in [the northern halves of Vermont and New Hampshire] indicated that poorer residents of amenity-rich nonmetropolitan areas often end up worse off as a result of the influx of persons from metropolitan areas. Their employment and income opportunities are too rarely improved as a result of the factors causing population turnaround.... The poor frequently feel the brunt of local price inflation and are denied access to recreation opportunities that they once took for granted, as more and more territory falls into the "off-limits" domain of the more affluent.

The New York Times reported[28] an example of this problem in Telluride, Colo. Five years ago Telluride was virtually a ghost town of 450 people, and Victorian houses were selling for $12,000. As its third ski season ended last spring, about 70 per cent of its 1,000 permanent residents were under 35 years old, and the same houses were going for $50,000. "Main Street is lined with adorable rustic bars and boutiques," the newspaper account continued. "The first Telluride Film Festival was held last summer. Telluride might just be only a few years away from becoming the kind of town its young escapists ran away from."

The new directions in rural migration mean that a far smaller number and proportion of the rural population is involved in farming, and this poses a threat to land conservation. An influx of people can lead to the despoliation of the environment. Vermont has enacted laws intended to stop the despoliation of the countryside but implementation is sometimes costly and unpopular locally. Property taxes have soared along with land values. The new movement back to the land is taking its toll among the old patterns of rural life. Protecting the countryside may mean compromising the absolute right to private property, since it presupposes central planning and limitations on the rights of ownership.

---

[28] April 16, 1975.

Urban-Rural Division of U.S. Population

Year	Urban population	Rural population
	(in thousands)	
1790	202	3,728
1800	322	4,986
1810	525	6,714
1820	693	8,945
1830	1,127	11,739
1840	1,845	15,224
1850	3,544	19,648
1860	6,217	25,227
1870	9,902	28,656
1880	14,130	36,026
1890	22,106	40,841
1900	30,160	45,835
1910	41,999	49,973
1920	54,158	51,552
1930	68,955	53,821
1940	74,424	57,245
1950	96,468	54,229
1960	125,269	54,054
1970	149,325	53,887

SOURCE: U.S. Census Bureau

Not all experts are equally certain that the figures on rural migration in the past few years point to a lasting trend. Demographers have pointed out, however, that when areas begin to gain or lose population, such movements tend to persist for a decade or two. The greatest threat to the continued increase in rural population would be a sudden, sizable change in the supply or price of gasoline since rural residents are more dependent on the automobile than city or suburban dwellers. Barring acute fuel problems, rural population growth is widely expected to continue at least into the 1980s.

Question of National Planning for New Growth

One question is whether this should take place haphazardly, as in the past, or as part of a national policy of population growth and distribution. "Overpopulation" problems are actually "the combined product of the population's size and its impact, magnified by rising consumption per capita, irregular age structure, and uneven distribution over the national territory," according to a study for the Commission on Population Growth and the American Future.[29] An abrupt downturn in the U.S. birthrate since 1970 and the movement away from metropolitan population centers have relieved some of these pressures. But even assuming a birthrate at only the replacement level, the population of the United States would reach 265.5 million in the year 2000, compared to 203.2 million in 1970, according to Census Bureau projections.[30]

Should national policies be evolved which would prevent further concentration, and perhaps even undo some of the concentration that has occurred over past decades? In Britain, France, Holland and Sweden government policies have aimed successfully at encouraging outmigration from congested centers.[31] However, there are many substantial barriers to such policies in America, ranging from the territorial interests of American legislators to conservative fears of federal intervention in local affairs.

Congress killed federal land use planning legislation for the foreseeable future July 15, when the House Interior Committee voted against reporting Rep. Morris K. Udall's (D Ariz.) bill. Land use legislation seeks to prevent random development and urban sprawl by encouraging states to classify land according to the way they want it used. Land use plans would have declared some areas open to development, set others aside for agriculture and restricted the use of places deemed environmentally important.

Udall's bill, like a Senate bill sponsored by Sen. Henry M. Jackson (D Wash.), authorized federal aid for states willing to undertake land use planning. No state would have been required to participate. Land use advocates say the federal government would not interfere in the substance of land use decisions, but simply would make sure there was a legitimate state planning process. Anti-land use forces, however, feared that the Interior Department would not declare a plan procedurally adequate unless it preserved a sufficient number of environmental areas. Congress' current preoccupation with ways to stimulate economic growth, especially in the hard-hit construction industry, also acted against land use legislation that was seen by some as limiting growth. Rep. Roy A. Taylor of North Carolina, one of three key Democrats who turned against Udall's bill in committee, asserted that the bill drew more grassroots opposi-

---

[29] Peter A. Morrison, "Dimension of the Population Problem in the United States," in *Population, Distribution, and Policy, op. cit.*, p. 7.

[30] For background on population projections, see "Zero Population Growth," *E.R.R.*, 1971 Vol. II, pp. 905-924.

[31] See "Protection of the Countryside," *E.R.R.*, 1971 Vol. II, pp. 541-563.

tion than any legislation he had seen during 15 years in the House.[32]

Vision of a Decentralized America of the Future

The "New Rural Society" project, headed by Dr. Peter C. Goldmark and funded by the Department of Housing and Urban Development,[33] envisions the use of communications technology to enable business and government to decentralize routine operations and transfer them to rural settings. In this brave new world of the future, the rural family would be connected to a job, school and stores via two-way cable television.[34] Electronic shopping could replace that symbol of old-fashioned rural America, the Sears Roebuck catalogue. The urban poor could be relocated to the newly revitalized countryside, helping to solve both their problems and those of the cities. Ideally, people would be able to choose whether to live and work in a rural or urban setting and still be confident of a satisfying life in either location, with jobs, health care, education and amenities at their fingertips.

Such ideas may never get beyond the point of science fiction. But the reopening of rural America is certain to have effects on city and country alike. In the 1976 presidential election, for example, it will be observed whether the urban newcomers have a liberalizing effect on their new neighbors, or whether the traditionally conservative atmosphere of the countryside will come to pervade their own beliefs.

In 1893 historian Frederick Jackson Turner wrote that "The existence of an area of free land, its continuous recession, and the advance of American settlement westward explain American development." A corollary to the Turner thesis, expounded in recent years, is that an urbanized America without a frontier outlet has turned bitterly inward. It may be that rural America will become a safety valve for the cities, and rural migration the means to the revitalization of both the countryside and the country.

---

[32] See *CQ Weekly Report*, July 19, 1975, p. 1520, and Mar. 1, 1975, pp. 428-432.

[33] Goldmark, now director of his own communications firm, was formerly the head of research at CBS Laboratories, and is especially known for his role in the development of the long-playing (LP) record.

[34] See "Cable Television: The Coming Medium," *E.R.R.*, 1970 Vol. II, pp. 669-686.

Selected Bibliography

Books

Borsodi, Ralph, *Flight From the City,* Harper & Row, 1933.

Cobb, Betsy and Hubbard, *City People's Guide to Country Living,* Macmillan, 1973.

Hansen, Niles M., *The Future of Nonmetropolitan America,* Lexington Books, 1973.

Nearing, Helen and Scott, *Living the Good Life: How to Live Sanely and Simply in a Troubled World,* Schocken Books, 1970.

Ogden, Samuel R. (ed.), *America the Vanishing: Rural Life and the Price of Progress,* Stephen Greene Press, 1969.

Sundquist, James L., *Dispersing Population: What American Can Learn From Europe,* Brookings Institution, 1975.

Taylor, Carl C., *et al., Rural Life in the United States,* Alfred A. Knopf, 1949.

Articles

Beale, Calvin L., "Rural Development: Population and Settlement Prospects," *Journal of Soil and Water Conservation,* January-February 1974.

Long, Larry H., and Kristin A. Hansen, "Trends in Return Migration to the South," forthcoming in *Demography,* November 1975.

McDonald, Susan S., "Flight Patterns," *National Review,* May 9, 1975.

"Out of the Cities, Back to the Country," *U.S. News & World Report,* March 31, 1975.

Wilson, Angela, "Emporium, Pa.: Life in a Small Town," *Ms.,* April 1975.

Wittner, Dale, "Return to Rural America: Seeking A Simpler Life," *Today's Health,* April 1975.

Reports and Studies

Beale, Calvin L., "The Revival of Population Growth in Nonmetropolitan America," report based on a paper presented at the Conference on Population Distribution, sponsored by the Center for Population Research, National Institutes of Health, January 1975.

—"Where Are All the People Going—Demographic Trends," paper presented to First National Conference on Rural America, April 1975, published by Rural America, Inc.

Bureau of the Census, U.S. Department of Commerce, "Mobility of the Population of the United States, March 1970 to March 1974," Series P-20, No. 273, December 1974.

"Demographic and Social Aspects of Population Growth" (Vol. I), and "Population, Distribution, and Policy" (Vol. V), research reports to The Commission on Population Growth and the American Future, Government Printing Office, 1972.

Editorial Research Reports, "Restrictions on Urban Growth," 1973 Vol. I, p. 85; "Mobility in American Life," 1973 Vol. I, p. 333.

Goldmark, Peter C., "The New Rural Society," The Communication Arts Graduate Teaching and Research Center, Cornell Univ., 1973.

Morrison, Peter A., "Urban Growth and Decline in the United States: A Study of Migration's Effects in Two Cities," Rand Paper Series P-5234, Rand Corp., May 1974.

UNDEREMPLOYMENT IN AMERICA

by

Mary Costello

July 11
1 9 7 5

UNDEREMPLOYMENT IN AMERICA

UNEMPLOYMENT has captured the national spotlight in recent months but, with a new crop of graduates in the labor force, a related problem is now receiving attention. This is the problem of underemployment—working at a job that does not make good use of one's ability, training or experience. Unlike unemployment, whose figures are compiled nationally each month by the U.S. Bureau of Labor Statistics (BLS), there is no official or objective measurement of underemployment. But its prevalence is well known. A study of working conditions conducted for the Department of Labor in 1974 found that 35 per cent of all American workers believed they were overqualified for their jobs.[1] Myron Clark, former president of the Society for the Advancement of Management, puts the figure at about 80 per cent.

As the demand for jobs, particularly professional jobs, continues to exceed the supply, the number of highly qualified persons working part-time at low wages continues to increase. According to BLS figures, the number of "subemployed" workers who wanted full-time jobs rose from 2.5 million in late 1973 to about 4 million in the spring of 1975. Employees at several companies are accepting pay cuts and reductions in the number of working hours to prevent large-scale layoffs.

Instead of moving on to better jobs, as they might have expected to do a few years ago, many workers are being forced to remain where they are. *U.S. News & World Report* has noted that "alongside millions of jobless workers, a new category of recession victims is appearing—men and women locked into jobs they would rather forsake for something better. Their career goals temporarily flattened under the weight of spreading unemployment, these 'immobilized workers' are holding onto whatever jobs they have until the unemployment climate brightens."[2]

There is another opinion that economic recovery will not cure or even significantly reduce underemployment. James O'Toole of the Center for Futures Research at the University of

---

[1] Robert Quinn, "1972-73 Quality of Employment Survey," University of Michigan Survey Research Center.
[2] *U.S. News & World Report*, April 14, 1975.

Southern California, for one, feels that the problems of underemployment "are basic and enduring shortcomings in the labor market and will not vanish with the current recession."[3] O'Toole's thesis is a gloomy one. It holds that throughout the industrial world there are too many educated men and women and too few good jobs suitable for their training and skills. As a result, many young people who grew up believing that education was the key to career success will be forced to take unchallenging jobs in which they have little interest and where the opportunities for advancement are slight. In the process, many of the less-educated workers will be displaced.

Bleak Employment Outlook for College Graduates

O'Toole is not the only Cassandra. The Bureau of Labor Statistics, in a recent survey of the job outlook through 1985, found that "problems for college graduates will more likely be employment below the level of skill for which they were trained, resulting in job dissatisfaction and high occupational mobility rather than unemployment." According to the bureau's projections, there will be 800,000 more college graduates in the labor force by 1985 than there will be new job openings for them—15.3 million graduates between 1972 and 1985 and 14.5 million jobs.[4]

While long-range predictions are by their nature subject to change, two recent studies found that college graduates in virtually all fields were having difficulty finding jobs today. The June 18 issue of Northwestern University's *Endicott Report* revealed that business demand for graduates with bachelor's degrees had declined by 31 per cent since the organization's November 1974 survey. Opportunities for holders of postgraduate master's degrees were down by 18 per cent. The findings, based on questionnaires sent to more than 100 of the nation's largest corporations, applied to engineering, accounting and business administration graduates as well as to those in the liberal arts.

A survey in May 1975 by the College Placement Council in Bethlehem, Pa., also indicated that demand for graduates was down this year. In November, employers in business, industry, government and non-profit and educational institutions—excluding teachers—had indicated to the council that they would be hiring about 4 per cent fewer college graduates in 1975 than in 1974. But by May the estimate was for an 18 per cent drop.

The occupations surveyed were (1) engineering, (2) sciences, math and other technical fields, (3) business, and (4) non-

---

[3] "Planning for Total Employment," *The Annals* of the American Academy of Political and Social Science, March 1975, pp. 73-74.
[4] "Occupational Manpower and Training Needs," 1974, p. 27.

Department of Labor
projections, 1972-85:

15.3 million college graduates
14.5 million jobs

technical or liberal arts specialties. "No categories escaped the downturn," the council reported. Engineering, after three successive years of increased hiring, fell 20 per cent. The least affected category was sciences, math and other technical fields, which dropped 7 per cent at the bachelor's degree level. Business declined 28 per cent. Job openings for liberal arts graduates fell 9 per cent "on top of a 45 per cent decrease in 1970-71 and almost no subsequent improvement in the intervening years."

Judging from their comments, the study reported, "employers do not expect appreciable improvement in hiring until possibly next spring." This time lag poses difficulties for recent graduates. Paul E. Steiger reported in *The Los Angeles Times* on June 1 that "a recurring nightmare" for some 1975 graduates is their fear that it will be five or six years before economic conditions will improve enough so that companies will be hiring in large numbers again. And by that time, he quoted Northwestern University graduate Greg Daugherty as saying, "instead of hiring those of us who have fried hamburgers and delivered mail for five years, waiting for things to get better, companies will recruit fresh college graduates."

Far more than their predecessors, today's college students are faced with the problem of finding a marketable specialty. A decade ago, they were encouraged to prepare for careers in medicine, law, engineering, science and teaching, and assured they would find good jobs in those fields. Subsequently nearly all of those fields became surfeited with graduates. Today the American Medical Association, concerned about an oversupply of doctors, is demanding that the influx of foreign physicians be halted. There are now about 30,000 law degrees awarded each year. But the Department of Labor estimates that there will be openings for only 16,500 lawyers a year during the 1970s.

Economic problems in the late 1960s and early 1970s brought about a large-scale retrenchment in engineering. The number of students choosing this field dropped sharply and by 1973 there was a shortage of engineers. The shortage soon turned into another surplus. The National Science Foundation projects that by 1985 more than 20 per cent of those holding doctoral degrees in engineering and science will be employed in areas unrelated to their specialty, compared to less than 10 per cent in 1972. And Professor Allan N. Cartter of the University of California at Los Angeles, one of the first to warn about a surplus of college teachers, now believes that less than 10 per cent of the new Ph.D.s will find teaching jobs in academe in the next few years.

The BLS predicts that there will be job openings for architects, geophysicists, computer specialists, chemists, accountants, employment counselors and health-related paraprofessionals in the next decade. These predictions are based on the assumption that the number of men and women choosing careers in these fields will remain relatively stable. But if past trends are any indication, it is likely that students will flock to these professions and that the job demand will soon outpace the supply. Thus the very forecasts tend to become self-defeating.

Entrapment Feelings in Secondary Labor Market

The oversupply of college graduates has an impact on the whole work force. As educated young people wait in line for jobs, workers already in the labor force are aware that employers would have little difficulty replacing them and thus they remain on jobs which, in another era, they would probably have left for more satisfying work. As opportunities for advancement and career mobility in many fields lessen, these workers are often left with a feeling of entrapment. The Bureau of Labor Statistics, in its 1974-75 "Occupational Outlook for College Graduates," said: "In the future, workers without college degrees will probably have fewer opportunities to advance to professional positions.... Thus, while college graduates may face competition for jobs, those without a college education will face even greater competition for the better jobs."

"Dual labor market" theorists see the economy divided into a primary high-wage sector and a secondary low-wage sector.[5] The two labor sectors are not precisely defined in terms of which jobs fall into what categories. While it can be assumed that the secondary sector is made up mostly of blue-collar workers, not all blue-collar workers are in the secondary sector. Skilled laborers in many fields receive high wages and numerous job opportunities. Studies have shown that the income gap between white and skilled blue-collar workers has narrowed considerably. This gap can be expected to narrow further as college graduates compete for scarce white-collar jobs.

"A basic fact about semi-skilled working-class life: it is on a flat level.... There is not too much point in working hard to get somewhere for there is no place to go."

Victor C. Gerkiss, *Technological Man* (1969)

Much that has been written about the work-related "blue-collar blues"[6] is directed primarily at unskilled or semi-skilled work. The feelings of apathy, dissatisfaction, discontent, entrapment and alienation ascribed to workers in relatively mundane jobs will surely become more pronounced if, as feared, college graduates are forced to accept employment that ignores their training and shatters their expectations. It has been shown that highly educated or intelligent workers in unchallenging and tedious jobs tend to be less productive and more accident-prone than their less gifted co-workers.

Women, blacks, the young and the old are overrepresented in unskilled occupations. William B. Werther Jr., an Arizona State University professor, describes the effect of their underemployment on job performance. "Even mature people in mundane jobs are likely to give less than optimal performance because the job

---

[5] See "Primary and Secondary Labor Markets: A Critique of the Dual Approach" by Michael L. Wachter in *Brookings Papers on Economic Activity*, No. 3, 1974, p. 639.
[6] See "Productivity and the New Work Ethic," *E.R.R.*, 1972 Vol. I, p. 293.

limitations are frustrating. This frustration must be relieved, and unexplained absences, horseplay or other irresponsible behavior are some of the ways that such frustrated feelings can be dissipated."[7]

Government Programs to Relieve Unemployment

Some see the solution to the problems of unemployment, subemployment and underemployment as the creation of thousands of public-service jobs. There are two basic types of public employment to combat these problems. The first, exemplified by Depression programs like the Works Progress Administration (WPA), focuses primarily on income maintenance for persons without jobs or with very low-paying jobs. The second, typified by many of the social programs during the 1960s, seeks to train persons with employment handicaps for permanent work.

The two major job programs of the 1970s sought to combine these approaches. The Public Employment Program (PEP), established under the Emergency Employment Act of 1971, and the Comprehensive Employment and Training Act (CETA) of 1973 were enacted to provide income maintenance for the unemployed "while emphasizing preferential consideration for members of special target groups (veterans, minorities and the disadvantaged) according to their representation among the unemployed."[8] These programs are intended as temporary relief until the economy improves.

In December 1974, Congress authorized $2.5 billion for state and local governments to hire unemployed workers for community-service jobs in education, health and day care, sanitation and recreation. In March, President Ford asked Congress for $2 billion to extend the public-service program for another year and to create more than 750,000 summer jobs. The bill Congress approved called for $5.3 billion; the President vetoed it as too inflationary. In June, Congress passed and Ford signed legislation appropriating $473 million for 840,000 summer jobs.

Public-service employment is often praised as a way of deriving needed public benefits from tax expenditures. But it is also regarded as an expedient rather than a long-term solution. James O'Toole wrote: "What kinds of jobs are being created? Not leaf raking perhaps, but jobs not likely to motivate the new generation of qualified workers."[9] A similar questioning of current public-service programs came from A. Dale Tussing, professor of economics at Syracuse University. Writing in the

---

[7] "Part-Timers: Overlooked and Undervalued," *Business Horizons*, February 1975, pp. 14-15.
[8] See "Manpower Report of the President," April 1975, p. 4.
[9] "The Reserve Army of the Underemployed," Part I, *Change*, May 1975, p. 32.

February 1975 issue of *Intellect* magazine, he observed: "To provide, through subsidized employment or direct public-sector hiring, still another set of low-paying, short-duration, dead-end jobs would make little if any contribution to the new unemployment. Instead, it is essential that the jobs created be of a long-term variety, contain a substantial on-the-job learning component, lead to possible advancement...."

Role of Education and Government

F ORMAL EDUCATION was not always viewed as the key to career success. Such industrial titans as John D. Rockefeller, Henry Ford and Andrew Carnegie had little schooling. Horatio Alger characters achieved success through hard work, clean living, and non-academic resourcefulness. Many of today's unemployed, underemployed or subemployed might well envy the opportunities that a bygone era seemed to offer anyone with the native intelligence and will to seize them.

The vast majority of 19th and early 20th century Americans were neither highly educated nor Horatio Alger successes. The rapid industrialization that followed the Civil War brought about a seemingly unending need for unskilled labor to man the factories and shops. "The workers who helped build this industrial empire often labored under harsh and hazardous conditions, lived in firetrap tenements, suffered unemployment and, even when working, received near starvation wages."[10] Employee discontent with wages, working conditions, long hours and unexpected layoffs led to often violent strikes and demands for unionization.

Most of the industrial workers were unskilled and uneducated; many were recent immigrants. High school was principally a preparation for college. In 1870, for example, 80 per cent of all high school graduates went on to college. College, in turn, led to a degree in the liberal arts and careers in law, medicine, teaching, the arts and some businesses. College graduates rarely had difficulty finding jobs in their chosen fields.

Beginning with the adoption of compulsory school attendance laws in many states around 1880, high school enrollment increased enormously. And as high school became the terminal point in the education of many young people, public demand for

---

[10] Jonathan Grossman and Judson MacLaury, "The Creation of the Bureau of Labor Statistics," *Monthly Labor Review*, February 1975, p. 21.

practical, career-minded education grew. Early vocational training programs were conceived as an attempt to "infuse new vitality into old curricula, to rouse student interest, to promote more sensible occupational choices, to raise the educational level of the laboring classes and to elevate all occupations to a millennium of culture and refinement."[11]

Academicians tended to be critical of efforts to train students for particular jobs. John Dewey, the philosopher and educator, attacked vocational education as undemocratic. The idea that a liberal arts education is the best preparation for work is still stressed by a number of American educators today. Typical of this thinking, University of Chicago President Robert Maynard Hutchins remarked in 1944: "The thing to do with vocational education is to forget it.... The task of the educational system is not to train hands for industry, but to prepare enlightened citizens for our democracy and to enrich the life of the individual by giving him a sense of purpose which will illuminate not merely the 40 hours he works but the 72 he does not."

Federal Government as Employer of Last Resort

Beginning with the Morrill Act of 1862, the federal government showed an interest in improving the skills of the labor force to meet the demands of technologically advancing agriculture and industry. The act provided the states grants of land to endow, support and maintain colleges to teach agriculture and the practical arts "to promote the liberal and practical education of the industrial classes." But until the depression of the 1930s, government concern with unemployment was directed toward the problems of supplying employers with needed workers rather than assuring working men of a sufficiency of jobs.

Massive unemployment forcibly turned the federal government's attention to a national problem of what to do with an idled labor force of unprecedented dimensions. By July 1932, wages were 60 per cent of their 1929 level, industry was operating at half the volume of 1929 and average monthly unemployment was running at 12 million, more than a quarter of the labor force. Many of those still employed were put on a shorter work week with less pay.

President Roosevelt, upon taking office on March 4, 1933, made unemployment relief one of the first orders of business. Over the next few years, millions of workers were hired and billions of dollars were spent on a host of programs. These included the Public Works Administration (PWA), the Civil Works Administration (CWA), the Federal Emergency Relief Administration (FERA), the Civilian Conservation Corps (CCC), the

---

[11] Grant Vern, *Man, Education and Work* (1964), p. 49.

National Youth Administration (NYA) and the Works Progress Administration (WPA).[12]

The best known and most controversial of these job-making programs was the WPA, established as an independent agency in 1935. It was a massive hire-the-unemployed project with the primary purpose of getting individuals and families off relief and putting them to work on socially useful jobs. Workers included the skilled and unskilled, professional and blue-collar. Over the eight years of its existence, WPA spent almost $11 billion and employed 8.5 million persons. Projects ranged from renovating 85,000 public buildings and constructing 16,000 water and sewer systems to writing an acclaimed series of state guidebooks. But the program's emphasis on income maintenance made it a target for criticism as "leaf-raking make-work."

At the end of World War II, however, there was widespread support for federal programs aimed at avoiding a repetition of the unemployment dislocations of the 1930s. President Truman on Sept. 6, 1945, called for "a national reassertion of the right to work for every American citizen able and willing to work" and "a declaration of the ultimate duty of government to use its own resources if all other methods fail to prevent prolonged unemployment." The next year, after protracted debate, Congress passed the Employment Act of 1946 which declared that "it is the continuing policy and responsibility of the federal government to use all practicable means...to promote maximum employment, production and purchasing power."

But Washington did little to create jobs for the unemployed during the first three postwar recessions, in 1948, 1953 and 1957. The first significant legislation came after the 1960-61 recession when unemployment approached 7 per cent, the highest since the Depression. The Manpower Development and Training Act (MdTA) of 1962, enacted to retrain workers with obsolete skills, put the government directly into job training. MDTA programs provided both on-the-job and institutional training for unemployed and underemployed adults and youth.

College Education Boom Following World War II

In the postwar recessions, unemployment and underemployment fell most heavily on the unskilled and undereducated. While these groups had always borne the major burden of employment dislocations, technological developments in the late 1940s and 1950s intensified the problem. As the demand for unskilled and semi-skilled workers waned, job opportunities for professional and other white-collar workers increased enormously.

---

[12] For background, see "Inflation and Job Security," *E.R.R.*, 1974 Vol. II, p. 707.

Ten Years of College Enrollments

Fall	Number of Students	Increase Over Prior Year
1974	10,321,539	6.5%
1973	9,694,297	4.3
1972	9,204,000	2.0
1971	9,025,031	4.3
1970	8,566,333	7.2
1969	7,978,408	5.4
1968	7,571,636	8.7
1967	6,963,687	8.2
1966	6,438,477	7.9
1965	5,967,411	12.2

SOURCE: U.S. Office of Education

Until the middle or late 1960s, the demand for skilled, educated workers seemed open-ended. Teachers, doctors, engineers, scientists, lawyers and other professionals generallly had a wide variety of jobs to choose from and ample opportunity to advance in their chosen careers. Education was almost universally accepted as the key to career mobility and the rising level of schooling for the population reflected this acceptance. In 1940, for example, only about 37 per cent of the workers aged 25-29 had graduated from high school; thirty years later, the figure had jumped to over 75 per cent. During that period, the percentage of 25-29 year olds with college or higher degrees rose from 5.8 per cent to 16.4 per cent.

The federal government encouraged the college boom. Under the Serviceman's Readjustment Act of 1944—the G.I. Bill—Washington provided veterans enrolled as full-time students a living allowance of from $75 to $120 a month and made direct payments to the institution for tuition, fees and other costs of up to $500 a month. Largely as a result of this program, male college enrollment jumped from 928,000 in 1945-46 to 1,659,249 in 1947-48.[13]

Congress reacted to the launching of the first Russian satellite, Sputnik I, in 1957 by passing the National Defense Education Act of 1958. That law provided scholarships, loans and grants to improve teaching in science, math and foreign languages. By the mid-1960s, attention shifted to the poor and disadvantaged in this country. Congress responded by enacting the Higher Education Act of 1965 which featured extensive aid

---

[13] See "College Recruiting," *E.R.R.*, 1974 Vol. II, p. 663.

for needy students and new programs of graduate study for public school teachers.

These programs plus the coming of age of the "baby boom" generation born after World War II resulted in a doubling of college enrollment in the 1960s—from 3,471,000 in 1959-60 to some 7,978,000 in 1969-70. Not only was there a large increase in the number of persons of college age, but the proportion going to college also rose. By 1970, 34 per cent of the 18-21 age group were enrolled in degree-credit programs in higher education, up from 23 per cent in 1960, 15 per cent in 1950 and 11 per cent in 1940.

Rising per capita income and growing social pressure to go to college contributed to the enrollment boom during the decade. Professor Paul Woodring, former education editor of the *Saturday Review*, wrote that a college degree had become a status symbol. "Both the students and their parents are convinced that the possession of such a document is essential if one is to achieve his goals in life." This belief, he added, "is rapidly becoming a part of the conventional wisdom. And to many the symbol has come to seem more important than the education it is presumed to represent."[14]

Job Shortages in Various Fields by Late 1960s

By the late 1960s, it had become evident that a college or graduate-level degree was not necessarily a ticket to a good job. Ivar Berg of Columbia University pointed out in his book *Education and Jobs: The Great Training Robbery* (1971) that almost four of every five college graduates were accepting jobs that had previously been filled by less-educated workers. A study by the Bureau of Labor Statistics in October 1972 showed that some 70,000 of the 750,000 persons who received college or graduate degrees the preceding June were unemployed. This was almost twice the national unemployment rate of 5.1 per cent. The study also showed that of those who found employment, many were in jobs virtually unrelated to their major studies in college. This situation applied to more than half of the humanities majors and to more than two-thirds of the business and social studies majors.

The very occupations that government programs had encouraged young people to enter a few years earlier were particularly hard hit. Unemployment or underemployment in science, engineering, teaching and business administration became apparent during the 1970 recession, the first since World War II in which large numbers of college-educated persons were thrown out of work. Toward the end of the year, 15 per cent of all business executives were estimated to be jobless. Due partly

---

[14] *The Higher Education in America: A Reassessment* (1968), p. 58.

to federal cutbacks in defense and space programs, 50,000 scientists and engineers were listed as unemployed in late 1970. Underemployment figures for these groups were believed to be considerably higher.

More publicized was the lack of job opportunities for teachers, particularly with doctoral degrees. Because of an anticipated decline in the number of professors needed in the next decade and an increase in the number of new graduates with Ph.D.s who wish to teach in college, their employment situation is not likely to improve. Many will be forced, like others immediately ahead of them, to find careers outside of academe. Some will compete for the dwindling number of teaching jobs in elementary and secondary schools. Others will settle for part-time teaching assignments which, according to Jane T. Flanders, a part-time lecturer in English at the University of Pittsburgh, "are marginal, expendable, underprivileged and underpaid."[15] Still others will try to find suitable work in private industry or government and, if all else fails, take temporary employment driving taxi cabs or tending bar. The majority will almost certainly be underemployed.

"Until we tell them [our young people]
that it is hopeless to look for fulfillment in
most of the jobs that are available to them,
we will be fooling them."

Chifton Fadiman, Council for Basic Education

The problems facing college graduates were summed up by William K. West, a 28-year-old graduate school dropout who recently lost his job at the New York City Planning Commission. "I've been overtrained for every job I've held, so eight years at a university cannot be justified in terms of the inculcation of skills necessary for work," he wrote. "Unfortunately, the society seems to have developed a whole class of people like me." Society, he continued, has produced "an entire class of intellectual day laborers, either out of work or severely underemployed —the mandarins who never were, more casualties of the misplaced optimism of the Sixties, of faulty social engineering."[16]

---

[15] Quoted by Malcolm G. Scully in *The Chronicle of Higher Education*, Jan. 20, 1975.
[16] Writing in *The New York Times*, June 18, 1975.

These men and women are not likely to take much comfort from President Nixon's Labor Day address to a joint session of Congress on Sept. 6, 1971: "No work is demeaning or beneath a person's dignity if it provides food for his table and clothes and shelter for his children."

Proposals to Relieve Underemployment

CAREER EDUCATION—training for the world of work—is seen by many as the best answer to the problems of underemployment and unemployment. The term "career education" was coined by former U.S. Commissioner of Education Sidney P. Marland in 1971. The goal of such training, Dr. Marland wrote in *Career Education: A Proposal for Reform* (1974), was that "all young people upon leaving the educational system...should be ready immediately to enter satisfying and useful employment in a field of the individual's choice."

Career-education proponents are quick to point out that the concept is much broader than the old vocational-training idea, which concentrated on giving potential high school dropouts the kind of skill that could lead to jobs in machine work or carpentry. In their view, career education should begin in elementary school where young people would be made aware of the world of work and given some idea of what a career involves. High schools would be structured to permit students some on-the-job experience.

The new vocationalists also favor the increasing number of on-the-job programs on college campuses. According to the National Commission for Cooperative Education, 900 four-year colleges now provide work-study programs, compared to only about 40 a decade ago. Almost 200,000 students are currently participating in these programs. With jobs scarce and unemployment high, career education has wide appeal. But criticism of both the practical and philosophical aspects of the concept has also grown.

In a book entitled *Public and Proprietary Vocational Training: A Study of Effectiveness* (1974), Welford W. Wilms of the University of California Center for Research and Development found that only about 20 per cent of the post-secondary vocational graduates who had trained for professional jobs found work in their field. Those who were hired earned 36 per cent less than non-vocationally trained college graduates doing

Career Education Boom

The number of secondary and post-secondary students and adults enrolled in vocational programs increased from 12 million in fiscal 1973 to almost 15 million the next year, according to the American Vocational Association. In fiscal 1973, the latest year for which figures have been broken down, 7.3 million participated in high school career courses, 1.3 million in post-secondary programs and 2.6 million in adult classes.

the same work. Another difficulty with career training was summed up by Henry M. Wriston, president emeritus of Brown University, in *The New York Times* on June 11, 1975: "Technology, and scholarship for that matter, move so swiftly that old jobs become obsolete and new ones arise for which specific 'preparation' is not available."

The Council for Basic Education objects to the tendency of career-education advocates to define education solely in terms of work. "Should only the student who has chosen the science career...study science?" the Washington-based council asked in its February 1975 *Bulletin.* "And what about history, foreign languages, mathematics and all the other subjects that we believe all young people should study? Must the school find a clear connection between these and the student's career goal to justify their place in his program?.... We believe that the sound goals of education far transcend a person's intended occupational career."

The differences between career and basic educators are not as irreconcilable as they might seem. The careerists are not advocating the substitution of specific market skills for basic learning; they want a combination of both, suited to the student's ability and career preferences. Basic educators believe that specialization should be built on top of a broad, liberal base and that needed skills can often be learned more easily on the job than in the classroom. They also contend that since there are not enough good jobs to go around, a well-rounded education can help workers make better use of their leisure time.

Attempts to Make Employment More Satisfying

"Society must rid itself of the delusion that the major purposes of education are to serve the economy and the economic needs of students," James O'Toole wrote. "Failure to do so will not only exacerbate the problems of underemployment; it will lead to a serious compromise of educational institutions."[17]

---

[17] "The Reserve Army of the Underemployed," Part II, *Change,* June 1975, pp. 60-61.

O'Toole sees underemployment as a continuing and incurable problem in the developed world and suggests several ways of relieving the dissatisfactions common among underutilized workers.

These include more flexible working conditions, job retraining and greater opportunities for part-time work and self-employment. Experiments in job flexibility have focused on the four-day week,[18] less structured working hours, more employee autonomy and increased participation in the decision-making process. Social psychologist Lars E. Björk described a 1971-72 experiment in flexible working conditions in a Swedish machine assembly plant in the March 1975 issue of *Scientific American* magazine.

"Most of us have jobs that are too small for our spirits."

Woman worker quoted by Studs Turkel
in *Working* (1974)

The traditional system, in which each of 12 men performed one specific operation, was replaced by a system in which the workers could allocate individual tasks, learn other jobs and use whatever methods they found most convenient and satisfying to complete the work. Björk reported an increase in productivity after the new system was installed. While admitting that work satisfaction is subjective and therefore difficult to measure, he concluded that "perhaps the most obvious sign of increased satisfaction is the fact that none of the men wanted to go back to the old system."

Some American companies are making greater use of part-time workers, sabbatical leaves and early retirements to lessen worker discontent and increase productivity. Particularly on routine jobs, part-timers are less prone to boredom and fatigue and therefore less likely to make errors. Pitney-Bowes of Stamford, Conn., which manufactures machines, postage meters and credit cards, allows two part-time workers to share one job. Xerox lets its employees take a year or two away from their jobs to work in public-service employment. Such innovations may well make some jobs less boring but it is questionable whether

---

[18] See "Four-Day Week," *E.R.R.*, 1971 Vol. II, pp. 607-626.

Graduates and Jobs

"A statistical 'oversupply' of college graduates does not imply that college graduates will experience significant levels of unemployment. The unemployment rate of college graduates has always been lower than that of workers with less education. Problems for college graduates will center on underemployment and job dissatisfaction."

—Bureau of Labor Statistics, "Occupational Outlook for College Graduates, 1974-75," 1974

they significantly reduce underemployment, particularly in white-collar occupations.

A growing number of workers are seeking to avoid underemployment and job dissatisfaction by going into business for themselves. Commenting on the increase in the number of young people starting new companies, Dora Dreiband of the New York County Clerk's Office said: "The youngsters just out of college, who are talented and well-educated, seem frustrated. Many don't feel like sitting around collecting unemployment or doing unskilled labor. So now the gutsy ones have been coming in a lot" to register to open a new business.[19]

Paradox of Job Openings Amid Unemployment

In addition to its public-service and manpower-training programs, the government has set up other projects to help the unemployed or underemployed find suitable jobs in their fields. Since 1968 the Department of Labor has operated Job Banks to compile lists of job openings and make the information available to city and state employment agencies. Even now, many available jobs go unfilled because of location, skill requirements or the unappealing type of jobs offered. Employment centers around the nation are reporting that droves of jobless work-seekers would rather continue to draw unemployment benefits than accept work they consider poorly paid, demeaning or beneath their ability.

At the same time, employers are reluctant to hire an "overqualified" applicant for fear that the person will quit the job at the first opportunity. Or they find that if a better job does not become available, the employee's frustration and unhappiness is likely to permeate his or her work and perhaps will soon be shared by other workers. In a survey of job opportunities around the nation published in *The New York Times* on July 1, 1975, Robert Lindsey wrote: "In a curious paradox of the nation's

---

[19] Quoted by Lawrence C. Levy in *The New York Times*, Feb. 23, 1975.

102

worst employment market since the nineteen-thirties, thousands of jobs go begging." He quoted Dorothy Graves, manager of the Southwest Pennsylvania Job Bank, as saying: "Anybody who is hard up and needs a job to eat can get work, even if they have no skills." But many of the jobs pay less than unemployment benefits and are regarded as menial or subservient.

Better methods for matching workers to jobs and improved forecasting are likely to have more of an effect on unemployment than on underemployment. The government now forecasts a slight increase in joblessness in the next few months and then a gradual reduction to about 8 per cent by the end of 1976. James O'Toole predicts that "whereas unemployment in the traditional sense will probably disappear in the U.S. in the future, the broader issue of underemployment will become more acute for all social classes because trends toward labor intensity and zero economic growth are likely to lead to a greater number of routine jobs."

Underemployment relief can come about in two basic ways. The first is the creation of many more good jobs that would use the skills and knowledge of an increasingly well-educated work force. The second, and probably more feasible, is a revolutionary change in the concept of work which might include greater job flexibility, options for career change and opportunities to move in and out of the labor force with more freedom than is now possible. If, as expected, the problems of underemployment and worker dissatisfaction grow in the years ahead, these and other alternatives are likely to be given more attention.

Unemployment in Two Decades

Sixties	Rate*	Seventies	Rate*
1960	5.5%	1970	4.9%
1961	6.7	1971	5.9
1962	5.5	1972	5.6
1963	5.7	1973	4.9
1964	5.2	1974	5.6
1965	4.5	Jan. 1975	8.2
1966	3.8	Feb. 1975	8.2
1967	3.8	Mar. 1975	8.7
1968	3.6	Apr. 1975	8.9
1969	3.5	May 1975	9.2
		June 1975	8.6

*Unemployment as a precentage of employment; monthly rates in 1975 are seasonally adjusted.
SOURCE: U.S. Bureau of Labor Statistics

Selected Bibliography

Books

Berg, Ivar, *Education and Jobs: The Great Training Robbery,* Praeger, 1970.

Ginzberg, Eli, *Manpower Agenda for America,* McGraw-Hill, 1968.

Howe, Irving (ed.), *The World of the Blue-Collar Worker,* Quadrangle Books, 1972.

Levitan, Sar A. and Garth L. Mangum, *Federal Training and Work Programs in the Sixties,* Institute of Labor and Industrial Relations, 1969.

Okun, Arthur M. (ed.), *The Battle Against Unemployment,* W.W. Norton & Company. 1965.

O'Toole, James, et al., *Work in America* Massachusetts Institute of Technology Press, 1973.

Turkel, Studs, *Working,* Pantheon, 1974.

Articles

Björk, Lars E., "An Experiment in Work Satisfaction," *Scientific American,* March 1975.

The Chronicle of Higher Education, selected issues.

Collins, Randall, "Where Are Educational Requirements for Employment Highest?" *Sociology of Education,* fall 1974.

Monthly Labor Review, selected issues.

O'Toole, James, "The Reserve Army of the Underemployed," Pt. I and II, *Change,* May and June, 1975.

"Planning for Full Employment," *The Annals* of the American Academy of Political and Social Science, March 1975.

Shaeffer, Ruth G., "The Buyers' Market for New College Grads," *The Conference Board Report,* February 1975.

Tussing, A. Dale, "Emergence of the New Unemployment," *Intellect,* February 1975.

Werther, William B., "Part-Timers: Overlooked and Undervalued," *Business Horizons,* February 1975.

Reports and Studies

Bureau of Labor Statistics, U.S. Department of Labor, "Expenditures and Manpower Requirements for Selected Federal Programs," 1975.

—"Occupational Outlook for College Graduates, 1974-75," 1974.

Carnegie Commission on Higher Education, "College Graduates and Jobs: Adjusting to a New Labor Situation," April 1973.

Council for Basic Education, selected reports.

Editorial Research Reports, "Education for Jobs," 1971 Vol. II, p. 845; "Inflation and Job Security," 1974 Vol. II, p. 707.

Gaines, Rilford, "Unemployment," Economic Report of the Manufacturers Hanover Trust Company, April 1975.

Keyserling, Leon H., "Full Employment Without Inflation," Conference on Economic Progress, prepared for the Task Force of the Commission on Full Employment, January 1975.

National Academy of Sciences, "Forecasting the PhD Labor Market: Pitfalls for Policy," April 1974.

U.S. Departments of Labor and Health, Education, and Welfare, "Manpower Report of the President," April 1975.

EDUCATION'S RETURN TO BASICS

by

Suzanne de Lesseps

**Sept. 12
1 9 7 5**

EDUCATION'S RETURN TO BASICS

A S THE FALL school term opens, there is a growing feeling among many parents that the public schools have not paid enough attention to the three traditional standbys—namely reading, writing and arithmetic. On one level, this feeling is related to dissatisfaction with the educational innovations of the 1960s and the belief that the schools have become too permissive. On another level, it is related to the growing mistrust of American institutions in general and the desire to recapture the stable, traditional values that have somehow gotten lost in the shuffle. "Some people are looking for greater regimentation," said Alonzo Crim, superintendent of schools in Atlanta. "As they view society in somewhat of a shambles, they feel a more conservative approach is better preparation for their young people."[1] "People are worried their children aren't respecting the old values," Bob Mackin, director of the National Alternative Schools Program at the University of Massachusetts, told Editorial Research Reports, "so they want to impose the basics on them."

The desire to return to traditional methods of teaching also goes hand in hand with the fiscal conservatism of the times. " 'Back to basics' implies things used to be better," said Dr. Vito Perrone, dean of the Center for Teaching and Learning at the University of North Dakota. "I don't think this is the case, but the slogan sells well in a time of recession."[2] According to a nationwide survey of school district budgets conducted by Market Data Retrieval, an educational research company based in Westport, Conn., the average cost of educating a student in the nation's public schools rose from $553.95 during the 1967-68 school year to $1,168.22 during 1974-75. Many parents are beginning to wonder if they are getting their money's worth. "As things begin to cost more, we tend to look at them more closely," said George Weber of the Council for Basic Education, a non-profit educational organization in Washington, D.C. "The public is getting more information on the outcome of innovative teaching methods and they're finding out the innovations aren't giving results."

---

[1] Quoted by Iver Peterson in *The New York Times*, March 3, 1975.
[2] Quoted by Gene I. Maeroff in *The New York Times*, April 20, 1975.

Weber also pointed out that parents have noticed an increase in disciplinary problems in the schools. "Rightly or wrongly, the public tends to associate discipline problems with poor academic performance," he remarked. In five of the last six years, Americans have regarded discipline as the biggest problem facing public schools, according to the annual Gallup Poll of Public Attitudes Toward Education.

In many parts of the country, parents are also upset by what they consider to be too much emphasis on the teaching of left-wing politics, sex education and street language. Violent protests erupted last fall in Kanawha County, W.Va., over the use of new textbooks that many parents regarded as un-American, blasphemous, critical of parental authority, immoral and obscene. One passage particularly irked them—it informed seventh graders that the idea that language is a divine gift is only one of six theories. Other examples of objectionable passages included readings from Malcolm X and other black writers; a poem by Roger McGough that depicted Christ as a beggar; an e. e. cummings poem that read "i like my body when it is with your body"; and a Gwendolyn Brooks poem that read "I think it must be lonely to be God/ Nobody loves a master...."

One West Virginia couple filed suit over the new textbooks, but U.S. District Judge Kenneth K. Hall ruled last January that the texts did not violate the principle of separation of church and state. As a result of the controversy, the Kanawha County school system has placed parents on textbook selection committees and adopted special selection guidelines that require, among other things, that new books not contain obscenity or mock the values of any religious or racial group. According to the new guidelines, English-language texts must contain instruction in the traditional rules of grammar.

Parent-teacher disputes have also arisen in Hanover County, N.C., and Baton Rouge, La., over the use of profanity in high school texts. In Prince George's County, Md., a film production of Shirley Jackson's short story "The Lottery," in which the winner is sacrificed to an unnamed deity, was banned because parents found it objectionable and blasphemous. Such controversies have not been limited to the South, however. Disputes over texts and teaching materials have erupted in such places as Aurora, Colo.; Syracuse, Ind.; McKeesport, Pa.; St. Paul, Minn.; Boise, Idaho; Grinnell, Iowa; and Neillsville, Wis.

Establishment of Fundamental Alternative Schools

From this dissatisfaction on the part of parents have emerged alternative public schools emphasizing educational fundamentals. They are now found in several cities. The National Alternative Schools Program at the University of Massachusetts has defined a public alternative school as one "which provides learning experiences not available in the conventional school, and which is available by choice and at no extra cost to every family within its community."[3] In the past, alternative schools were set up to give students more freedom and a broader curriculum. The new alternative schools, however, emphasize strict discipline and the traditional "three R's."

The John Marshall Fundamental School in Pasadena, Calif., perhaps the best known of the new "fundamental" schools, was established in 1973 after the election of three conservative school board candidates who promised to end court-ordered busing and return discipline to the schools. John Marshall provides a basic curriculum with emphasis on arithmetic, reading drills and social studies. Rigorous homework assignments are given, and students are graded by the traditional letter system. Students attend flag-raising ceremonies every morning, recite the pledge of allegiance in class and follow a strict dress code. Character training is stressed and students may be spanked or kept after school for bad behavior.

"Inability to be firm is to my mind the commonest problem of American parents today."

Dr. Benjamin Spock
Raising Children in a Difficult Time (1974)

The John Marshall School, which houses grades K (kindergarten) through 12, was so popular that the district school board opened a second fundamental elementary school, Sierra Mesa, in the fall of 1974. It is run in the same manner as John Marshall—homework in all grades (including kindergarten), strict discipline, and emphasis on the basics. Several children at Sierra Mesa have had their mouths washed out with soap for misbehavior. Such measures seem to enhance the school's popularity. According to Dorothy Fagan, director of information and communications for the Pasadena Unified School District, there are 1,600 students on waiting lists for the district's two fundamental schools.

Two other schools similar to John Marshall and Sierra Mesa have opened in suburban Jefferson County, Colo., outside of

---

[3] National Education Association, "Briefing Memo on Alternative Schools," August 1974, p. 2.

Denver. In Cupertino, Calif., six classes in the Panama Elementary School, corresponding to grades one through six, participate in the Academics Plus (A+) program that emphasizes competition, the Golden Rule, academic drills, dress codes and letter grades. According to Mrs. Harrell Bell, a member of the Academics Plus Committee, A+ is scheduled to expand to a second Cupertino elementary school this fall.

Interest in the Basics Among Minority Groups

In Charlotte, N.C., the school district responded to pressure from parents for more structure and discipline in the public schools by converting Myers Park Elementary School into an alternative traditional school. The principal, Lewis L. Walker, acknowledged to *Nation's Schools and Colleges* magazine reporter Jane S. Shaw that there may have been underlying motives in setting up the school. Myers is situated in an affluent white section of Charlotte, and many parents were able to avoid having their children bused to schools farther away. However, this school is required by court order to have a black student population of at least 20 per cent. "Since we've gotten out and talked to black parents, we've found that many are interested in the traditional concept," said Walker last year. "In fact, it seems that many people of both races are ready for the schools to head back on a middle road in education."[4]

According to Dorothy Fagan, there has been a "definite interest" in the fundamental schools within the black community in the Pasadena area. This fall the school district plans to open a fundamental program in kindergarten in a black neighborhood school. The following year, the program is scheduled to be extended through the third grade. "One of the phenomenons of the program is that both alternative schools are integrated and it's on a voluntary basis," said Pasadena Superintendent Frank Cortines last fall.[5]

Parents of poor minority-group children are often the first to understand the need for a solid education. "They see education as a way out," said Frances Quinto of the National Education Association. "They realize that only through education can they get out of the cycle of poverty." Doreen H. Wilkerson has written in her book *Community Schools*: "[The poor child] must learn those skills and acquire that knowledge which will tend to give him a fairer share of the good life and a stronger voice in his own destiny. This means a strong emphasis on the basic tools of civilized society: reading, writing and critical analysis."[6] Ac-

---

[4] Quoted in the Council for Basic Education *Bulletin*, October 1974, p. 3.
[5] Quoted by B. D. Colen in *The Washington Post*, Nov. 21, 1974.
[6] Doreen H. Wilkerson, *Community Schools* (1973), p. 46.

cording to a recent survey by *The New York Times*, the parents of black and Hispanic children in large urban school systems are demanding an emphasis on basic skills.

Decline in Test Scores of High School Students

In the meantime, pressure for more emphasis on the basics at the elementary and secondary level has come from the colleges. Increasingly, the colleges have complained about entering freshmen who are deficient in basic reading and writing skills. "In general...students coming to Stanford—to any college, really—do not know how to write very well," said Fred Hargadon, dean of admissions at Stanford University. "They have not had to do so in high school for the most part.... Criticism of students' writing ability comes from college faculties everywhere. Admissions officers readily concur...."[7] Last fall, officials at Bowdoin College in Maine estimated that more than 10 per cent of the freshmen lacked basic skills in English. Admissions Director Richard W. Moll said high schools had stressed the "fun and the relevant" social science courses at the expense of composition, math and reading. "The result," he said, "is that a good many bright students are quite conversant with local, national and international problems, but they can't write three consecutive declarative sentences in the English language."[8]

Test scores on the College Entrance Examination Board's Scholastic Aptitude Test (SAT)—a test that is given to help forecast how a high school student will perform in college—have fallen steadily during the last 13 years for which results are available. The average verbal score has declined from 478 in 1962-63 to 434 in 1974-75; tests are scored on a scale from 200 to 800. The average math score has also dropped every year, although not as much, from 502 in 1962-63 to 472 in 1974-75. Scores on tests administered by the American College Testing Program (ACT) have also fallen during the last 10 years for which data are available. The average composite score has declined from 19.9 in 1964-65 to 18.7 in 1973-74, although it has not fallen every year. The ACT scale ranges from 1 to 36.

Lillian Weber, a professor at City College of New York who helped bring informal education to the United States from England, has argued that the "open, learner-centered" innovations in elementary education should not be held responsible for the apparent decline in student achievement. "These kids who are not achieving now in high schools and colleges never even had open education," she said. "It was the end of the 1960s before the schools were really doing anything in open

---

[7] Quoted in *Parade*, March 2, 1975.
[8] Quoted in *Newsweek*, Oct. 21, 1974, p. 91.

Declining National Test Scores

	SAT[1] Score Averages		ACT[2] Score Averages
School Year	Verbal	Mathematical	Composite
1962-63	478	502	NA[3]
1963-64	475	498	NA[3]
1964-65	473	496	19.9
1965-66	471	496	20.0
1966-67	467	495	19.4
1967-68	466	494	19.0
1968-69	462	491	19.4
1969-70	460	488	19.5
1970-71	454	487	18.9
1971-72	450	482	18.8
1972-73	443	481	18.9
1973-74	440	478	18.7
		472	NA[3]

[1] Scholastic Aptitude Test. Scale ranges from 200 to 800.
[2] American College Testing Program. Scale ranges from 1 to 36.
[3] Not Available.

SOURCE: College Entrance Examination Board and the American College Testing Program.

education, and at that time it was a drop in the bucket. We're not the ones producing what people are complaining about."[9] Weber was supported in her assertion by Bob Mackin. "Elementary open education wasn't available to kids now in college," he said in an interview. "Even now, there are about 100,000 to 125,000 kids in open, alternative programs, which is minuscule when compared to the number of kids in the entire educational system."

Major Trends in American Education

THE IDEA of an open educational environment, in which children are allowed to explore a wide assortment of subjects at their own rate, was borrowed in the 1960s from the infant schools in Britain[10] where the informal approach had caught on after World War II. Supporters of this educational theory believed that every child should experience school for its

[9] Quoted by Gene I. Maeroff in *The New York Times*, April 20, 1975.
[10] Roughly comparable to primary-grade schools in America.

own sake and not merely as a preparation for something later on in life. In his book *Crisis in the Classroom, Fortune* writer Charles E. Silberman described an informal elementary classroom typical of the ones he visited in England in 1968. "To photograph an informal classroom for infant and younger junior school children, one needs a motion-picture camera with sound, for the initial impression is that the children are all in motion," he wrote. "At any one moment, some children may be hammering and sawing at a workbench, some may be playing musical instruments or painting, others may be reading aloud to the teacher or to a friend.... Elsewhere in the room...there are likely to be children seated at a table or sprawled on the floor, writing a story."[11]

"The theory that each pupil should be allowed to choose his own subject matter and work at his own rate is absurd.... Too many lazy little monsters opt for the easiest courses...."

Patrick W. Guiney, math teacher
in New York state public schools

A year before Silberman's visit, a Parliamentary commission called the Plowden Committee had publicized the informal approach of many of the infant schools and recommended that it be instituted in all English primary schools. Shortly thereafter, Lillian Weber began her work to establish informal schools in New York City. She founded the Advisory Service to Open Corridors that advised teachers who wanted to institute the change, and she organized the Workshop Center for Open Education for anyone interested in informal education. Credit for bringing the new approach to the United States should also be given to the Education Development Center of Newton, Mass., which supported several open education groups. It was the Silberman book, however, that heightened public interest in the British infant system and stimulated the open education movement in the United States. "Informal education can work as well in the United States as in England," he proclaimed. "This flat assertion is based on experience as well as theory...."[12]

---

[11] Charles E. Silberman, *Crisis in the Classroom* (1970), p. 223.
[12] *Ibid.*, p. 266.

Standard, teacher-centered class

It is difficult to know how many open classrooms there are in the United States today. Most of the older alternative schools across the country use the open, informal approach, and many aspects of this approach have filtered into conventional classrooms. A recent survey conducted by Roberta Weiner, an education professor at Adelphi University on Long Island, found that 60 per cent of the responding 184 schools on the island had open classrooms. Officials at 19 per cent of the schools said more than half of their classes were open and 10 per cent said all of their classes were open. "It would be useful if a national survey were conducted to ascertain the full scope of the movement," wrote Harold W. Sobel in a recent issue of *Phi Delta Kappan,* a professional educational journal.[13]

Philosophy Behind Student-Centered Learning

The theory behind open, individualized education is grounded in the works of many philosophers, including Jean Jacques Rousseau, Friedrich Froebel, John Dewey and Jean Piaget. Their ideas on education span three centuries, beginning with Rousseau's writings in the 18th century. Froebel is credited with introducing the idea of kindergarten in 1837 and Dewey is known as a leading theorist of progressive education in America. Piaget, a contemporary Swiss psychologist, is sometimes called "the giant of the nursery." He formulated the theory that a child's activity plays a primary role in his mental and

---

[13] Harold W. Sobel, "Is Open Education a Fad?" *Phi Delta Kappan,* April 1975.

...Modern, student-centered class

educational development, since a child constructs reality out of his own experiences.[14]

This theory had been advocated before, particularly by Dewey, who maintained that schools should be "embryonic social communities," fostered by society's values and full of activity. He wrote: "When the school introduces and trains each child of society into membership within such a little community, saturating him with the spirit of service, and providing him with the instruments of effective self-direction, we shall have the deepest and best guaranty of a larger society which is worthy, lovely, and harmonious."[15] In 1896, Dewey established the experimental Laboratory School, which followed no definite curriculum, at the University of Chicago.

Dewey's thoughts and ideas strongly influenced members of the new "progressive movement" in education that began as a protest against the narrow formalism in schooling during the late 19th century. "Progressive education began as part of a vast humanitarian effort to apply the promise of American life...to the puzzling new urban-industrial civilization that came into being during the latter half of the nineteenth century," wrote Lawrence Cremin. "The word *progressive* provides the clue to what it really was: the educational phase of American Progressivism writ large."[16] The progressive educators viewed

---

[14] See David Elkind, "Piaget," *Human Behavior*, August 1975.

[15] "The School and Society" (1899), reprinted in *John Dewey on Education* (1964).

[16] Lawrence Cremin, *Transformation of the School* (1960), p. viii.

the school as an instrument to help students achieve self-realization and adjust to the rapid changes of society. In 1919, the Progressive Education Association was founded, and in 1924 its quarterly publication, *Progressive Education,* began to publish articles about many different kinds of educational experiments.

Deemphasis of Traditional Academic Subjects

One result of the progressive movement was that public schools broadened their curricula to include such non-academic subjects as home economics, physical education and vocational training. The schools began to place more emphasis on the social and emotional development of students and less on such traditional academic subjects as mathematics, literature, history and languages. In 1918, the National Education Association's Commission on the Reorganization of Secondary Education issued a statement in which it formulated what it thought to be the primary goals of American schools.

The commission emphasized that the needs of students who did not go on to college should not be forgotten and that more attention should be paid to the different talents and attitudes of individual students. "Moreover," wrote Richard Hofstadter, "the child was now conceived not as a mind to be developed but as a citizen to be trained by the schools. The new educators believed that one should not be content to expect good citizenship as a result of having more informed and intellectually competent citizens but that one must directly teach citizenship and democracy and civic virtues."[17]

Although the *number* of students studying academic subjects in high school increased from 1900 to 1950, the *percentage* of students studying them declined. In 1910, 49 per cent of the public high school students studied Latin. By 1949, this figure had fallen to 7.8 per cent. In the same period, enrollments in modern languages dropped from 84.1 to 22 per cent; mathematics from 89.7 to 55 per cent; and science from 81.7 to 54.1 per cent. Eventually, many academicians and parents began to worry that too little attention was being paid to basic subjects. Demands for more academic rigor increased after World War II as college entrance standards rose and admission became more difficult.

By the 1940s, the progressive movement in education was losing its appeal. In 1955, the Progressive Education Association was unable to attract members and was forced to dissolve. "The progressive movement in education had been in part a victim of its own success," wrote Paul Woodring, "because its best

---

[17] Richard Hofstadter, *Anti-intellectualism in American Life* (1963), p. 335.

features—an emphasis on understanding the nature of the child as an individual, the use in the classroom of psychological knowledge gained during the first half of the century, a freedom from repressive discipline and the employment of student interest as a motivation for learning—had, by 1950, become standard practice in many schools and hence were no longer considered 'progressive.' "[18]

Major Currents in Education From 1955 to 1965

In 1955, public interest in the teaching of reading was aroused with the publication of Rudolf Flesch's book *Why Johnny Can't Read*. His best-seller attacked the "look-say" method of instruction—the child is taught to recognize whole words and phrases from their general appearance—as primarily responsible for the poor reading performance of elementary school children. He argued for phonic instruction in which the child begins by learning the sounds associated with letters and letter combinations. "According to our accepted system of instruction," Flesch wrote, "reading isn't taught at all. Books are put in front of the children and they are told to guess at the words or wait until Teacher tells them."[19] Many of Flesch's critics accused him of being a sensationalist who exaggerated the shortcomings of reading instruction and offered an over-simplified cure for all reading problems. Flesch's defenders argued that he was compelled to resort to shock treatment to bring a serious problem to the public attention.

Two years after the appearance of Flesch's book, the American education establishment was thrown into a frenzy with the Russian launch of Sputnik I, the first man-made earth satellite. Suddenly, Americans realized they were behind in the space race and something had to be done to catch up. In 1958, in an attempt to close the gap, Congress passed the National Defense Education Act to provide scholarships and grants to improve math, science and foreign-language instruction. The act also provided for the development of audio-visual aids in the classrooms, such as tape recorders and television. Guidance counseling was stressed because of its importance in identifying gifted youths.

In an attempt to upgrade the educational system and to reach more students, many new teaching techniques were instituted during the late 1950s and early 1960s. "We innovated all over the place," wrote John I. Goodlad, dean of the graduate school of education at the University of California, Los Angeles, "with new approaches to curriculum content; with programed and

---

[18] Paul Woodring, *Investment in Innovation* (1970), p. 89.
[19] Rudolf Flesch, *Why Johnny Can't Read* (1955), p. 17.

computerized instruction; with modular scheduling, modular buildings, and acoustically treated walls, ceilings and floors; with nongrading, team teaching, and flexible grouping; with films, film strips, multimedia 'packages,' and televised instruction."[20]

Government aid to education increased rapidly during the 1960s with the passage of legislation supporting research, fellowships, traineeships and special building projects. For the first time in U.S. history, Congress approved federal scholarships for needy undergraduates by passing the Higher Education Act of 1965. The Elementary and Secondary Education Act of 1965 provided financial assistance for education programs, such as the pre-school "Headstart" project, aimed at increasing the opportunities of disadvantaged children in city slums and rural areas. Title III of the act embodied the idea of "innovative" education which had grown very popular by this time.

Post-Sputnik Introduction of 'New' Mathematics

Sputnik provided an impetus for changes in the teaching of physics, chemistry and biology. Students were encouraged to learn to discover the sciences by experimenting rather than by memorizing formulas and theorems. Mathematicians began to question the traditional curriculum and to search for better ways of teaching the discipline. The "modern" or "new" math sought to broaden the understanding of mathematics among students by introducing them to the fundamental principles and theories behind the subject. "Conceptual insight" was a favorite phrase used by mathematicians to describe the goals of the new curriculum. Students of the new math were introduced to set theory, the concepts of union and intersection, and the associative, distributive and commutative laws. They were also taught how to compute in base systems other than base 10.

In recent years, as mathematical test scores have declined, the new math has fallen into disfavor in many quarters. Confused parents have become frustrated over not being able to help their children with their work. Critics have charged that too little time was spent teaching the standard mathematical skills and that teachers were not properly prepared for the new curriculum. Others, such as Morris Kline, author of *Why Johnny Can't Add* (1973), have argued that topics like Boolean algebra, symbolic logic and abstract algebra were too advanced for young students.

A recent study conducted by the National Assessment of Educational Progress (NAEP) has provided new evidence that

---

[20] John I. Goodlad, "An Emphasis on Change," *American Education*, January-February 1975, p. 21.

young people are lacking in basic computational skills. The NAEP tested about 34,000 17-year-olds and 4,200 adults (ages 26-35) and found that:

> Only 10 per cent of the 17-year-olds and 20 per cent of the adults correctly calculated a taxi fare.

> Only 1 per cent of the 17-year-olds and 16 per cent of the adults were able to balance a checkbook.

> Less than half of both groups could determine the most economical size of a product.

> Forty-five per cent of the adults could not read a federal income tax table correctly.

J. Stanley Ahmann, former NAEP director, speculated that the new math might be responsible for the poor rate of performance since it stressed abstract theory more than practical application. "Too many students apparently fail to see the relationship between math courses in school and the use of math in everyday living," said Roy H. Forbes, the project's new director.[21] Despite much of the criticism of the new math, many instructors have felt that some of its aspects have a great deal to offer students since it does help them understand how and why mathematical computations work. The pendulum is not expected to swing all the way back to rote memorization of tables, and many teachers have begun to adopt the best features of the new math.

Some Current Directions in Pedagogy

WHILE THE "back to basics" movement has often been thought of as right-wing, it should be noted that many schools across the country have begun to stress the fundamentals without adopting a conservative emphasis on discipline, patriotism and dress codes. One school which appears to have combined the best of traditional and progressive approaches to teaching is the alternative Hoover Elementary School in Palo Alto, Calif. The school was opened after a group of parents called for a return to traditional basics. A moderate amount of homework has been given in all grades at Hoover and weekly progress reports have been sent to parents every Friday. Report cards, complete with letter grades, have been given every quarter, and no student has been promoted without mastering the required work.

Officials at Hoover believe that the best way for a student to build a positive self-image is through solid academic

---

[21] Quoted by Eric Wentworth in *The Washington Post,* July 25, 1975.

achievement, beginning with the basics. Yet "nothing about the school smacks of the rigidities one associates with the perennial call for a return to the old verities and the Three R's," Fred Hechinger wrote last January. "At a first glance the only noticeable difference from any other school was an air of courtesy and a low level of noise. The children seemed less frantic and appeared relaxed rather than regimented or submissive."[22]

Meanwhile, the state of California has begun a program called Early Childhood Education (ECE) aimed at making sure that all primary students achieve competence in basic subjects. The program involves students from all types of economic backgrounds, not just the poor. During the last school year, 280,000 school children, 22 per cent of the total number of pupils in kindergarten through third grade, were involved in ECE. The program has been expanded to include 33 per cent this fall.

The Early Childhood Education program appears to be in keeping with the philosophy of California Gov. Edmund G. Brown Jr. He has indicated he wants to concentrate money in the elementary grades rather than in non-traditional educational ventures. In a recent interview with Don Speich of the *Los Angeles Times*, Brown said he considered adult education and external degree programs "interesting" services rather than "survival" services. Later on, he added: "I suggest that we ought to examine the question of whether or not we ought to direct more [money] at the earlier ages.... If people get the skills and get off on the right footing maybe some of these things that are now packaged for later stages in a person's life will not be as necessary...."[23] According to Walter Denham, administrator for elementary education program planning in California, "Brown favors ECE over many other programs" because it is aimed at restructuring and reforming the elementary school system.

The rationale of the ECE program is that it enables teachers to detect and correct learning difficulties while the child is young, thereby avoiding massive remedial instruction on a higher level. To achieve this goal, instruction is tailored to the individual needs of each student. A personal profile outlines each child's strengths and weaknesses in all skills, particularly in reading and mathematics.

One interesting feature of ECE is the degree of parental involvement in the program. Because the adult-student ratio in the program is required to be one to ten, volunteers are recruited

[22] Fred Hechinger, "An Experiment with Tradition," *Saturday Review*, Jan. 11, 1975, p. 58.
[23] *Los Angeles Times* story distributed to and published in the Louisville *Courier-Journal & Times*, Aug. 3, 1975.

in large numbers. Last year, ECE schools hired 8,000 aides and used 23,000 volunteers including parents, grandparents and college students. Parents help devise goals and teaching plans and thus have a voice in what their children are being taught.

Acceptance of Individualized Instruction Methods

The trend toward individualized instruction, the key to the ECE program, was stimulated by scientific research during the past 20 years that gave educators and psychologists new insight into the learning process. Researchers have documented the fact that different individuals learn at varying rates of speed, and that some approach learning analytically and others intuitively. New research has shown how small children discern language sounds, and educators have been able to divide reading skills into different units, such as word construction, comprehension and vocabulary.

Many elementary schools use an individualized approach to reading in which students are allowed to progress at their own pace. Even at the fundamental school in Pasadena, teachers are encouraged to pay attention to the individual needs of each student. Anna Mary Hession, director of the district's elementary curriculum, singled out one teacher who epitomized the goals of John Marshall: "She is very creative, constantly evolving new ideas. She assesses the level of where the children are and individualizes her teaching. And she has much human warmth and affection for every one of her students."[24]

Opponents of the fundamental schools have emphasized that they are not against this type of teaching at all. In fact, the teacher described above might fit very well into an open classroom. What they have warned against, however, is what they consider to be the reactionary philosophy behind some elements of the movement, such as the emphasis on dress codes, patriotism and rigid discipline. Even the Council for Basic Education, which has always emphasized the importance of the basics, has issued a call for restraint. "We think the 'basic' alternative schools should be selective about what they recapture from long-ago education," stated a recent issue of the Council's *Bulletin*. "Emphasis should be on knowledge, not on the way students dressed, or marched single file to recess. Some aspects of modern education have proved useful in solving learning problems for individual students, and we wouldn't want this progress to be lost in an attempt to bring back the Class of 1915."[25]

---

[24] Quoted by Jane S. Shaw in "The New Conservative Alternative," *Nation's Schools & Colleges*, February 1975, p. 33.

[25] Council for Basic Education *Bulletin*, May 1975, p. 14.

Frances Quinto of the National Education Association stated that setting up a separate, fundamental school with a certain set of values had the potential of polarizing the community and the students. "Society and life are not rigidly structured," she said. "There is a mobility and ease about things in this world. We have freedom and free choice. If we take children out of this enviornment and then put them in a back-to-basics school, with a rigid atmosphere, I don't know if it will work at all." Bob Mackin of the National Alternative Schools Program agreed with Quinto's assertion that students should be offered a variety of options. "What's good for one kid may not be good for another," he said. "A community should offer many alternatives, including the free school, the open school, the fundamental school, evening school, vocational schools and schools that focus on one specific field such as science. It's not an either-or situation."

Examples of a Pluralistic Approach to Education

One example of a school district that has offered elementary students a great deal of choice is Long Beach, N.Y. The district has provided three separate elementary school programs: one fairly rigid and traditional; one liberal and open; and one in the middle. In San Geronimo, Calif., the district's two elementary schools also have offered three programs: an open alternative, the regular school program, and a third program called Advance Basic Capabilities (ABC) that has stressed testing, discipline, and basic skills.

At Quincy II High School in Quincy, Ill., students have been able to choose from five different subschools. The students first must undergo a planning and evaluation session with parents, teachers and administrators. Quincy II has offered a traditionally structured school; a more liberal classroom program for motivated students who wish to draw up their own curriculum; a more flexible school for those in between; a fine arts school for students interested in music, art and theater; and finally a vocational school for those who want to pursue careers in such fields as nursing, computer programing, business and auto mechanics.

In his book *Public Schools of Choice*, Mario Fantini, dean of education of the State University of New York at New Paltz, outlined his proposal for the establishment of many choices within one public school system. Operating on the principle that parents should be allowed to choose a school that suits their child's needs best, Fantini described seven different options that one community could develop, ranging from the "free" learner-centered classroom to the standard institution-centered classroom. Fantini argued that parents, teachers and administrators need to get away from the idea that "one, rather mono-

Controversy Over MACOS

A course of study that has angered many parents across the country is called "Man: A Course of Study" (MACOS). It is currently being offered in about 1,700 schools nationwide with the aid of funds from the federally supported National Science Foundation. Parents are upset over a segment on the Netsilik Eskimos that, they claim, espouses cultural relativism and undermines Western moral values. They argue that fifth graders are much too young to be exposed to a culture that engages in wife-swapping, cannibalism, adultery and infanticide.

MACOS supporters maintain that the course is intended to help children understand their own "humanness" and promote cultural understanding. They deny any attempt at indoctrination. But Dr. Rhoda Lorand, a child psychologist at Long Island University, contends that children are forced to identify with the Netsilik value system through role-playing and reenactment of Eskimo myths.

Since MACOS is funded by the National Science Foundation, the controversy has extended to include the larger question of federal involvement in educational curricula. Rep. Olin E. Teague (D Texas), chairman of the House Science and Technology Committee, has initiated a General Accounting Office audit of the program and has appointed a special curriculum panel to study the matter.

lithic education process" must be made to work for everyone. "Teachers...ought to be encouraged to develop alternative forms that are congruent with their own styles of teaching...and so increase significantly the chances for educational productivity," Fantini wrote. "This is especially likely to occur if the same alternatives offered teachers are made available to students—by *choice*. Such decisions not only increase consumer satisfaction, but also offer new learning opportunities to students who are not responding well to the standard option."[26]

As the pendulum continues to swing toward more traditional pedagogic methods, educators are hoping that the idea of continued improvement through educational research and development will not be pushed aside. "The task of the 1970s is not to go *back* to the basics; on the contrary, the task is to use well-planned programs of educational improvement...to move *forward* to basics," said Samuel G. Sava, vice president of the Charles F. Kettering Foundation, last November.[27] This past summer both the NEA and the National School Boards Association warned school districts around the country to expect more disputes over textbooks and teaching material this year. Clearly, the question of how to give parents a greater choice in the type of school their children attend is more important than ever.

[26] Mario Fantini, *Public Schools of Choice* (1974), p. 248.
[27] Speech to the Annual Conference of the Association for Individually Guided Education, Chicago, Nov. 16, 1974, reprinted in *Vital Speeches*, Jan. 15, 1975.

Selected Bibliography

Books

Fantini, Mario, *Public Schools of Choice*, Simon and Schuster, 1974.

Flesch, Rudolf, *Why Johnny Can't Read*, Harper & Row, 1955.

Gross, Beatrice and Ronald, editors, *Radical School Reform*, Simon and Schuster, 1969.

Hofstadter, Richard, *Anti-intellectualism in American Life*, Alfred A. Knopf, 1963.

Kline, Morris, *Why Johnny Can't Add*, St. Martin's Press, 1973.

Silberman, Charles, *Crisis in the Classroom*, Random House, 1970.

Woodring, Paul, *Investment in Innovation*, Little, Brown and Company, 1970.

Articles

"Back to Basics in the Schools," *Newsweek*, Oct. 21, 1974.

Elkind, David, "Piaget," *Human Behavior*, August 1975.

Hechinger, Fred, "An Experiment with Tradition," *Saturday Review*, Jan. 11, 1975.

Goodlad, John I., "An Emphasis on Change," *American Education*, January-February 1975.

Nyquist, Ewald, "Nontraditional Approaches," *Today's Education*, November-December 1974.

"Reforms That Went Sour in Teaching the Three R's," *U.S. News & World Report*, May 20, 1974.

Sobel, Harold W., "Is Open Education a Fad?" *Phi Delta Kappan*, April 1975.

Shaw, Jane S., "The New Conservative Alternative," *Nation's Schools & Colleges*, February 1975.

Studies and Reports

American College Testing Program, "Trends in the Academic Performance of High School and College Students," Richard L. Ferguson and E. James Maxey, July 21, 1975.

Council for Basic Education, *Bulletin*, selected issues; "Uses and Abuses of Standardized Testing in the Schools," George Weber, May 1974.

Editorial Research Reports, "Reform of Public Schools," 1970 Vol. I, p. 279, "Educational Equality," 1973 Vol. II, p. 645.

McCandless, Sam A., "The SAT Score Decline and Its Implications for College Admissions," paper presented at the 1975 Western Regional Meeting of the College Entrance Examination Board, January 1975.

National Assessment of Educational Progress, *Consumer Math*, selected results from the first national assessment of mathematics, June 1975.

National Education Association, "Alternatives in Education," Infopac No. 8, August 1974.

FUTURE OF WELFARE

by

Helen B. Shaffer

**Nov. 21
1 9 7 5**

FUTURE OF WELFARE

T HE "WELFARE MESS" is the nation's most enduring domestic issue, a classic battlefield in American politics for the clash of conservative and liberal ideologies. Packing as much political dynamite today as it did 10 and 20 years ago, welfare is bound to figure prominently once more as an issue in the national election campaign of 1976. President Ford has called for a cutback in welfare spending and his challenger for the Republican nomination, Ronald Reagan of California, wants the responsibility for all welfare and related programs transferred from the federal to the state governments.

The National Governors' Conference, in contrast, has taken a stand in favor of full federal financing of a minimum income standard for the entire population every year since President Nixon proposed such a plan in 1969. The threatened bankruptcy of New York City, attributed in large part to the heavy drain on its budget of extensive and relatively generous social-welfare programs, has intensified concern in all states where other cities with large welfare burdens are located. Payments to its one million welfare recipients cost New York City $48.34 for every man, woman and child in the city in 1974. A study by the private, non-partisan Citizens Budget Commission, released on Nov. 16, indicates that this amount still represented only 30 per cent of the entire welfare cost in New York City. The state and the federal government paid the rest.

Like his three immediate predecessors in high office, President Ford has felt compelled to direct attention to questions of welfare reform and the 94th Congress can expect an administration proposal on this subject shortly after its second session convenes in January. A special task force appointed by the Domestic Council in the White House has been studying the welfare situation, and other domestic problems, over much of the past year with a view to presenting the President with available options for action he might take or recommend to Congress to overcome defects of the system. Meanwhile hundreds of bills to change this or that phase of the nation's welfare machinery are before Congress, as they have been before previous sessions for many years back. A growing consensus, however, has come to favor complete overhaul and simplification of the entire system.

Although a sizable part of the population is on the receiving end of one or more of the government's social welfare programs *(see opposite page)*, the problem of poverty persists and tax-payers chafe at the expense. Dissatisfaction with the welfare situation has been made worse by recurring charges of waste, fraud, and administrative error. Inflation and unemployment plus warnings of economic dangers in federal budget deficits all contribute to keeping the "welfare mess" on the political griddle.

That a democratic and affluent nation cannot afford to ignore the basic human needs of its people is a generally accepted proposition. But neither conservative nor liberal critics of the welfare system have been able to resolve a basic dilemma—how to provide for those who cannot support themselves without penalizing low-income wage-earners, encouraging the growth of a dependent class, and devoting too large a proportion of national income to the support of non-producing parts of the population. The problem is partly technical (how to regulate the total economy so as to minimize poverty and its attendant problems), partly political (how to win support for a particular system, or reform of a system of social welfare), and partly moral (how far the government should go toward providing relief of human privation).

Ford's Attempt to Reduce Social Welfare Spending

Pressure for reform of welfare emanates from two basic positions: One is that welfare has grown too big, applies to too many persons, and puts too great a strain on the national economy. The other is that the system is unwieldy, inefficient, and unfair. The moves toward reform, therefore, move along these two tracks which sometimes overlap.

The Ford administration has stressed the need to reduce the welfare burden on the economy. Its main argument is that the nation cannot afford to spend so much of its income for social purposes. In a typical statement of his position, President Ford told the National Federation of Republican Women, Sept. 13, he was determined to reverse a trend in social spending that "literally threatens our whole economy." He would veto "again and again and again" any bills enacted by Congress to enlarge the social-welfare spending. If this spending continued at its present rate of expansion, he warned, "by the year 2000 half the people of this nation will be living off the other half."

Ford offered a tax proposal on Oct. 6 based on the same premise. The President asked Congress to enact a permanent tax cut amounting to $28 billion and to reduce government spending by an equal amount. Although he did not specify the budget items, there was little doubt from other actions and

Recipients of Income-Support Programs*

Social Insurance**

Social Security
Old Age Retirement 27,244,000
Disability 4,125,000
Railroad Retirement 1,019,000
Federal Civil Service 1,393,000
Veterans 5,485,000
"Black Lung"*** 485,000
Unemployment Insurance 4,774,550

Medicare:
Bills for in-patient hospital
stay, Jan.-April 1975 2,532,000
Bills for doctors' and related
services, Jan.-May 1975 35,753,000

Supplemental Security Income

Aged 2,326,330
Blind 73,849
Disabled 1,788,323

Public Assistance*

Aid to Families with
Dependent Children 11,367,000
(children: 8,114,000)
General Assistance 995,000
Emergency Assistance 41,400

* As of June 1975 except for public assistance and unemployment insurance figures, which date from April 1975
** Includes dependents and survivors
*** Benefits to miners, dependents and survivors under Federal Coal Mine Health and Safety Act of 1969

SOURCE: Social Security Administration

statements that his intent was to reduce spending for social programs, including welfare.[1]

Congressional Study of System's Shortcomings

The second line of attack on social welfare is that the system is inefficient and counterproductive. These thoughts have been voiced with increasing force from both conservative and liberal critics. The major defects of the system were summed up and documented a year ago by a subcommittee of the Joint Economic Committee of Congress at the conclusion of an intensive, three-year investigation and analytic study of the nation's welfare situation. Most of the criticisms since then have echoed

---

[1] A Treasury Department analysis of his tax proposal, made at the request of *The New York Times*, indicated that low-income families would be worse off under the Ford tax-cut plan than under rebate provisions of tax law in effect in 1975.

the findings of this subcommittee.[2] The most serious short-comings of public welfare cited by the subcommittee were:

Fragmentation. "The habit of approaching problems in isolation has led to fragmented and inconsistent legislation and administration." Income security programs alone "are shaped by at least 21 committees of Congress and by 50 state legislatures, by six cabinet departments and three federal agencies, by 54 state and territorial welfare agencies...by more than 1,500 county welfare departments, by the U.S. Supreme Court and many lesser courts." The result is that official action, whether legislative or administrative, never addresses the welfare problem as a whole. Yet action on one segment of the system inevitably affects other segments.

Inequity. The system favors individuals who fall into particular categories—the old, the disabled, fatherless children, etc.—but ignores or shortchanges others equally in need. Variations in state and local benefit levels and in eligibility rules compound the unfairness. To illustrate one of the many aspects of inequity, the report noted that 57 per cent of all payments for Medicaid *(see Glossary, p. 135)* are made in states with only one-fourth of the poverty population, while states with one-half the poverty population disburse only 19 per cent of Medicaid funds. A Census Bureau study indicated that one-half of the public assistance payments in 1972 went to families and individuals whose incomes, together with welfare aid, were above the officially defined poverty line.[3] At the same, more than one-third of the nation's families in poverty received no cash assistance at all.

Unreliable adequacy standards. Since there is no consensus on what an adequate standard of assistance should be, this is a fertile field for political debate. The answer depends on what a nation can afford, what the effects of different benefit levels will be on the welfare of all, and what the influence will be on the probability that the recipient will eventually become self-supporting. "The more 'adequate' the benefits for some, the more inequitable is the system to those...ineligible to receive any benefits at all."

Disincentives for self-support. By establishing categories of persons eligible for public assistance, the system is said to encourage the growth of these categories. A case in point is the unmarried teen-age mother who is encouraged by the system to establish a separate home, thus becoming eligible for Aid-to-Families-with-Dependent-Children (AFDC) benefits, rather than remaining with her family, completing her schooling, and preparing for self-support. Another unfortunate effect is the encouragement of fathers to desert their families so the mother and

---

[2] Subcommittee on Fiscal Policy of the Joint Economic Committee of Congress, *Income Security for Americans: Recommendations of the Public Welfare Study*, Dec. 4, 1974. Sen. William Proxmire (D Wis.), a member of the subcommittee, described this report as "the result of the most thorough and thoughtful analysis of our welfare program...ever...undertaken."

[3] $4,275 a year in 1972 for a family of four; $5,050 in 1975.

children can qualify for AFDC. Loss of benefits due to an increase in earnings is another disincentive to self-support.

Duplication and error. A "continuous stream of regulations from Washington and state capitals that incorporate new law, new administrative policies, new court decisions" confuse case workers and applicants alike. "Each welfare program...requires separate arithmetic for each family or individual enrolled." Work rules for mothers of dependent children differ for AFDC and food stamp eligibility. A gain from one aid program may reduce or eliminate the benefit from another, possibly with a net loss to the recipient. A boost in Social Security income for an aged recipient might cost that person far more in loss of Medicaid.

Errors in Administering the Welfare Programs

The discovery of costly errors in administering welfare programs has led to the institution of several so-called "quality control" measures to weed out ineligibles and eliminate over-payments. A campaign of this kind was aimed at the AFDC program after a six-month sample survey in 1973 showed errors that had occurred in determining eligibility or payment in four out of 10 cases. The Department of Health, Education, and Welfare (HEW) then ordered the states, which administer AFDC with the help of federal grants, to reduce the errors or suffer the penalty of losing federal aid. The goal was an error rate of no more than 13 per cent: 3 per cent in determining eligibility and 5 per cent each for errors of over- or under-payment. Corrective action was begun on Jan. 1, 1974. Eight months later, HEW announced that the effort in the first half of the year had reduced the overall error rate from 41 to 37.9 per cent.

Results of another HEW study, released May 12, 1975, showed $500 million had been paid out erroneously in 1974 despite quality control efforts. Much of the error was due to failure to adjust eligibility or payments levels as family circumstances changed, such as an increase in other income or attainment of age 18 by a dependent child. The campaign continued, however; the states took such precautions as checking state employment records, requiring more frequent income reports from recipients, and substituting flat grants for variable sums based on case worker evaluations of each case, the latter having proved more error-prone. Twenty-three states now use flat grants for AFDC cases.

The campaign paid off in terms of savings. HEW announced on Oct. 31, 1975, that during the first 18 months of the drive, from January 1974 to July 1975, "quality control" had saved the federal and state governments $411 million in AFDC payments and unknown amounts in costs of medical and other services that might have been accorded to ineligible recipients. Some 109,000 cases involving 270,000 individuals had been removed from the rolls. Overpayments had been corrected in 209,000 cases and underpayments in 73,000. There was still a distance to go to meet the efficiency goals, however. Only seven states[4] brought errors concerning eligibility down to 3 per cent, and only two states (Nevada and North Dakota) were below the 5 per cent goal on overpayments. Underpayment was much less prevalent; 21 states met the accuracy goal.

Another embarrassment involving costly errors hit the welfare establishment with the disclosure that the government had been overpaying recipients of Supplemental Security Income (SSI). This program was begun Jan. 1, 1974, to replace the old Public Assistance but serves the same clientele, the needy aged, blind, and disabled. Under the new program these aid recipients technically are taken off the relief rolls and made beneficiaries of the Social Security system. Their benefits are financed entirely by federal funds.[5] Social Security Administration (SSA) data, submitted to the House Ways and Means Committee in June 1975, indicated that approximately 13 per cent of the SSI cases had been overpaid. At that time there were about four million SSI beneficiaries, and they received an average of $157 a month.

In response to a number of questions put to him in writing by Sen. Birch Bayh (D Ind.), SSA Commissioner James B. Cardwell reported on Sept. 28 that the agency had identified overpayments totaling $460.8 million during the first 18 months of the program, through June 30, and that the figure might rise higher. The average overpayment was around $26.60 a month. From past experience, the government could expect a prompt rebate from about 14 per cent of the recipients and repayment in installments from 25 per cent. But some of the overpayments were written off because the individual amounts were too small to make the collection effort worthwhile.

Charges of Abuse in Availability of Food Stamps

Still another welfare-linked scandal of the past year concerned the growth of the food stamp program, which today serves more than 19 million persons at a cost of $6 billion a year. This program, administered by the Department of Agriculture, provides stamps at discount prices for the purchase of food at retail outlets. Anyone eligible for public assistance is eligible to purchase food stamps. Others qualify on the basis of family size and income. For example, a family of four may receive stamps worth $162 a month in food purchases. These stamps may cost the family nothing if its net income is less than $20 a month, or as much as $138 if the family's net income has reached $540 a month.

---

[4] Indiana, New Jersey, Oklahoma, South Dakota, Texas, West Virginia and Wisconsin.
[5] States may voluntarily supplement these payments, however.

Critics of the program have complained that because of a liberal policy on allowing deductions in computing net income,[6] families earning as much as $16,000 a year and college students living away from their relatively affluent families were qualifying for stamp purchases. Secretary of the Treasury William A. Simon called the program "a haven for...chiselers..."[7]

The Ford administration moved in the fall of 1974 to reduce food stamp benefits as part of a general domestic budget-cutting campaign. The move set off a stream of protests from labor and consumer groups. Congress, by overwhelming majorities in both houses, voted in February 1975 to block a Department of Agriculture plan for cutting the food stamp subsidy. A U.S. Court of Appeals, acting on a suit brought by activist groups, ruled on June 12 that the department's stamp allotment plan was illegal and that a new formula should be drawn up that would give all poor families an opportunity to purchase a nutritionally adequate diet.

To meet the court's objections, the department has proposed changes that would give consideration to the age and sex of each member of a family or raise the allowance for larger families. These proposed changes in regulations were published in the *Federal Register* Sept. 19 for the filing of comments by interested individuals or groups until Nov. 13. While these matters were going on, numerous bills have been introduced in Congress to amend the food stamp program. Sen. Herman E. Talmadge (D Ga.), chairman of the Senate Agriculture Committee, has called the program "an administrative nightmare." A bill he is sponsoring reflects the White House view.

Growth of Income-Support Benefits

F ROM ITS EARLIEST beginnings, public assistance to the poor has been governed by two mutually modifying principles: (1) that a community is morally and socially obliged to provide the necessities of life to those who lack them, and (2) that the assistance given should never be so pleasing that the recipient will prefer it to self-support. Much of the piecemeal growth of welfare in modern times has been the result of efforts to push various parts of the system in one direction or the other—to be more generous to the poor, or to diminish the attractions of dependence on public bounty.

---

[6] Among the deductibles—business expenses, union dues, mortgage payments, tuition and training expenses, taxes including Social Security taxes.

[7] Junior Achievement National Conference, Bloomington, Ind., Aug. 12, 1975.

Popular irritation over welfare today derives a good deal from the feeling—justified or not—that the existing system violates the second principle. Two centuries ago Thomas R. Malthus argued against the English poor laws of his day, not because of their harshness but because they encouraged the poor to be indolent, to marry and breed children, thus enlarging the poverty problem.[8] A century ago, the New York Society for the Prevention of Pauperism said that "reliance upon charitable aid...must unavoidably tend to diminish in the minds of the labouring classes that wholesome anxiety to provide for the wants of a distant day...." In our time, a Secretary of Health, Education, and Welfare has warned that "when there are so many inducements to go on welfare, there is no real incentive to leave..."[9]

Basic Question of Charity or Earned Right

Part of the impetus toward the founding of the various social insurance systems in our day was to ease the dilemma presented by the contrary motivations of public assistance. It was hoped that by establishing various contributory programs, the potentially poor—the orphaned, the unemployed, the old, the retired, the disabled—would receive support in time of need as a matter of earned right, thus eliminating difficult questions of policy on public charity. As the programs developed, eligibility as a matter of earned right and eligibility as a matter of human need became intertwined. Reform of public welfare programs to help the poor therefore cannot be detached from consideration of the benefits (and costs) of such other public programs as Social Security, Medicare and veterans' benefits.

The earliest public assistance programs in colonial America followed the lead of the English Poor Laws and, like them, served not only a humanitarian but a social purpose in ridding the community of beggars and the banditry associated with roving bands of homeless, unemployed men. "The 'beggars' were the characteristic evil of the 16th century [the century the first poor laws were enacted—in 1536, 1547, 1572 and 1576]" writes the English historian G.M. Trevelyan. Among them were former ploughmen cast off from agricultural employment by enclosure of lands for grazing. In addition, suppression of the monasteries had eliminated an important source of alms and set adrift large numbers of monastic servants. "The 'beggars' became the objects of both fear and pity."[10]

As in the mother country the New England colonies required each locality to support its indigents, established residence re-

---

[8] See his *Essay on the Principles of Population As It Affects the Future Improvement of Society*, published in 1798.

[9] Caspar W. Weinberger, speech to the Commonwealth Club of San Francisco, July 21, 1975. Weinberger left office as HEW Secretary Aug. 10 succeeded by F. David Matthews.

[10] G. M. Trevelyan, *History of England*, Vol. II (1953), pp. 31-32.

Glossary of Welfare Terminology

AB. Aid to the Blind, a public assistance category.

AD. Aid to the Disabled.

AFDC. Aid to Families with Dependent Children, largest of the federally supported public assistance programs.

FAP. Family Assistance Plan, name given to President Nixon's proposal in 1969 to provide a national income floor for all poor families and individuals.

Medicaid. Program to finance medical services for the needy.

Medicare. Health service financing system under Social Security.

Negative Income Tax. Tax plan whereby individuals and families whose incomes are below a federally defined poverty line receive an amount sufficient to bring their incomes up to that line.

OAA. Old-Age Assistance.

OASDI. Old-Age and Survivors and Disability Insurance, the basic Social Security program providing monthly benefits to retirees.

Supplementary Security Income. New program of benefits to needy aged, blind, and disabled persons, replacing earlier public assistance programs for those categories.

Vendor Payments. Payments made by a social service agency for medical or other services rendered to beneficiaries of social service programs.

quirements for aid (to discourage itinerant begging) and required the able-bodied to work for their pittances. Paupers, including juveniles, were often bound over under contract to individuals who used them as apprentices or a form of indentured labor. Later on, workhouses and "poor farms" were established, where conditions were such that only those in the most desperate circumstances would apply for help.

Early Debate on Institutional vs. Home Relief

By the mid-19th century, the debate on welfare centered mainly on the relative merits of "indoor relief" (poorhouse) and "outdoor relief" (aid, often in the form of food and goods, to those living at home). The Guardians of the Poor of Philadelphia opposed outdoor relief in 1827 because it was "calculated...to blunt and ultimately destroy that noble pride of independence, the birthright of every American...[and] promotes idleness and not infrequently crime." On the other side, a New York Senate committee, favoring outdoor relief, urged in 1857 that "worthy indigent persons should, if possible, be kept from the degradation of the poorhouse by reasonable supplies of provisions, bedding and other absolute necessaries at their own homes."[11]

---

[11] Lucy Komisar, *Down and Out in the U.S.A.: A History of Social Welfare* (1973), p. 24.

Aid was most readily given to widows and orphans. Mothers' pension laws, first adopted in Missouri and Illinois in 1911, provided monthly payments for poor widowed or abandoned mothers. Next in line of favored treatment were the aged and the blind. When the Depression struck in the 1930s, almshouses were still the most prevalent source of aid for the penniless. Ten states had no outdoor relief at all, and several states still had laws for contracting out the labor of the indigent and for the apprenticeship of pauper children.

New Deal View of Government's Responsibility

The sheer size of the Depression and the millions rendered destitute by unemployment of the family breadwinner forced a new approach to the problem of public assistance.[12] With private charity unable to cope with the magnitude of the need, public action on a large scale became inevitable. An Emergency Relief and Construction Act of 1932, providing federal loans to states for work relief, was not adequate to meet the crisis.

Shortly after President Roosevelt took office in March 1933, Congress enacted the Federal Emergency Relief Act (FERA)—the first national public assistance law. Under this measure, some 18 million Americans received cash stipends in small amounts, averaging in 1933 around $15 a week per family. In addition, a federal Surplus Relief Corporation was established to purchase surplus food and distribute it to the needy. The Works Progress Administration (WPA), a job-creating agency, replaced FERA in 1935 at a time of bread lines and hunger marches and complaints about inadequacies and defects of the relief system. The Depression experience weakened the concept that poverty resulted from personal inadequacy, and it propagated the idea that the root cause was a malfunctioning of the economic system. From this view came the belief that the government was obliged to take significant action beyond providing mere handouts to the needy.

The Social Security Act of 1935 set the pattern for what has remained the structural foundation of social welfare in the United States. The act provided insurance for the unemployed and the retired, and public assistance for three categories of persons likely to be unable to earn a living for themselves: the aged, the blind, and children in homes without breadwinners—the disabled were added later. The social insurance features were in direct response to Depression conditions which had deprived the normally self-supporting persons of earned income.

The public assistance features reflected the growing approval of helping the needy remain in their own homes rather than

---

[12] By 1932, one-sixth of the working population was jobless and many cities were facing bankruptcy.

placing them in institutions. One carryover from the past was that the public assistance programs stayed under state administrative control, although the federal government was now providing much of the funds. The amounts given were low, even by Depression standards, but it was a start. When Old-Age Assistance (OAA) went into effect in 1936, the average monthly grant was $18.67.

From the beginning, the "something-for-nothing" programs have not been popular except in cases of dire need suffered by obvious victims of a cruel fate. Since the early New Deal days, charges of fraud, waste, inefficiency and misuse of tax money for political advantage have dogged the public assistance programs. Roosevelt, whose New Deal created the income-support structure, was no friend of relief. "Continued dependence upon relief induces a spiritual and moral disintegration, fundamentally destructive to the national fiber," he said in 1935.[13] The expectation of the founders of the system was that the social insurance programs ultimately would underpin family income and that public assistance would shrink to a minor program providing for the irreducible remnant of destitute persons.

Expansion of Welfare Role; Anti-Poverty Aims

Over the years, the basic insurance system was amended again and again in the direction of greater coverage and liberality of benefits—but so was the public assistance program. In 1950 the disabled were added to relief rolls, "vendor payments" to doctors and other suppliers of medical services to the needy were instituted, and mothers or other caretakers of dependent children became eligible for support payments in addition to the children, with ADC thus becoming AFDC. A decade later, in 1961, unemployed fathers became eligible for the federal-aid program on option of the states; 23 states now provide support under this category. Maternal and child health benefits, first authorized under the 1935 Social Security Act, were enlarged from time to time. Funds to help pay the medical expenses of public assistance recipients were authorized in 1950, and 11 years later a new category of medical aid—Medicaid—was provided for the "medically indigent"; that is, for those not poor enough to qualify for public assistance but too poor to pay their medical bills.

Meanwhile, enlarging amendments to the social insurance programs tended to give these programs some responsibilities that formerly rested with public assistance. In 1939, dependents and survivors of insured workers became eligible for benefits. In

---

[13] Quoted by Henry Hazlitt, *The Conquest of Poverty* (1973), p. 87. See also Arthur Schlesinger Jr., *The Age of Roosevelt: The Coming of the New Deal* (1958), p. 296.

Public Fund Expenditures* for Social Welfare
(in millions)

	1950	1960	1970	1974
Social insurance	$5,000	$19,300	$54,700	$98,500
Public assistance**	2,500	4,100	16,500	33,600
Health-medical	2,000	4,500	9,700	14,000
Veterans	6,900	5,500	9,000	14,000
Education	6,700	17,600	51,000	72,800
Housing	15	177	700	2,600
Other social welfare***	447	1,140	4,400	7,000
Totals	$23,500	$52,300	$146,000	$242,400

*Includes capital outlay and administrative expenses
**Plus medical payments and social services
***Includes vocational rehabilitation, child nutrition and welfare, institutional care and other programs

SOURCE: Department of Health, Education, and Welfare

1956 benefits were extended to workers who become disabled before they reach normal retirement age. In recent years, Congress has increased Social Security benefit schedules several times, and there is now an automatic cost-of-living escalator built into the benefit system.[14]

The 1960s were marked by a growing realization that poverty for many persons was a trap for which public assistance and related programs provided no escape hatch. Welfare reform was then directed in large part toward efforts to rescue the poor from chronic dependency. This was the thrust of President Johnson's "war on poverty," first announced in a message to Congress in January 1964, then implemented later that year with passage of the Economic Opportunity Act. The act provided for a number of programs emphasizing rehabilitative services, pre-school education, training and jobs for young people, retraining for older underemployed persons, and self-help. Inadequate financing, deflection of White House interest to the Vietnam War, and hostility by local officials were among the obstacles to the success of the programs. In an era of civil unrest, marked by riots in the black ghettos of many cities, the "war on poverty" lost its steam. It was finally dismantled in the early years of the Nixon administration.[15]

The overall effect of the developments over the past 40 years

[14] See "Retirement Security," *E.R.R.*, 1974 Vol. II, pp. 967-984.
[15] See "Future of Social Programs," *E.R.R.*, 1973 Vol. I, pp. 251-268.

has been a great growth of social welfare coverage and expenditures. The number of recipients of all the various cash-income support programs reached 44 million in 1974, doubtless with some overlapping due to multiple benefits for some retirees. The total outlay for cash benefits alone under these programs totaled $112.4 billion that year.[16] The expenditure of tax funds for both cash benefits and services amounted to $242.4 billion *(see box, opposite page).*

Social welfare expenditures increased by an average of 11 to 13 per cent a year during the early 1970s. Among these expenditures, public assistance grew markedly faster than other forms of social welfare, as is shown in the following table drawn from Social Security Administration data:

Program	1971-1972 Increase	1972-1973 Increase	1973-1974 Increase
Social Insurance	12.7%	15.1%	14.4%
Public Assistance	22.6	10.0	17.2
Health-medical	13.8	1.7	11.2
Veterans	10.2	13.0	7.5
Education	6.4	7.7	11.5
Other	12.7	11.4	9.5

The dependent children program accounts for most of this rise. Despite a declining national birthrate, the number of recipients on relief is two and a half times higher than it was 10 years ago *(see table, p. 140).* In some cities as many as one-third of the children are supported at least in part by AFDC payments. In terms of total expenditures, the most costly of all public assistance programs is Medicaid.

Prospect of Overhauling the System

THIS VAST NETWORK of income-support programs has become too interlocked into the economy of the nation and too enmeshed in the bureaucratic procedures of federal, state and local governments to permit significant reform without considerable dislocation. How far reform should tamper with the basic design is a debatable question. While it is widely agreed that the system has defects, there is also recognition of its overwhelming benefits. If it has not eradicated poverty, at the very least it has kept afloat millions who might otherwise

---

[16] "Current Operating Statistics," *Social Security Bulletin,* October 1975.

Growth of AFDC* Program

	Number of Recipients**	Total Payment (federal and state)
1950	2,233,000	$ 554,000,000
1960	3,080,000	1,063,000,000
1965	4,396,000	1,644,096,000
1970	9,659,000	4,857,000,000
1971	10,653,000	6,230,447,000
1972	11,069,000	7,019,621,000
1973	10,815,000	7,211,431,000
1974	11,006,000	7,918,113,000
1975	11,303,634	7,402,000,000 est.
1976	——	9,460,000,000 est.

*Aid to Families with Dependent Children, ADC prior to 1962
**Number in December of each year except 1975 when the June figure was used

SOURCE: Social and Rehabilitation Service, Department of Health, Education, and Welfare

have become destitute or have suffered intolerable privation. Moreover, it has been a means of redistributing national income to those in the lower economic brackets, greatly enhancing their purchasing power. This function has had an incalculable effect on the economy.

Changing Policy as to Employment of Mothers

Recent amending legislation reveals a change of policy toward women in the AFDC program. They are encouraged, even required, to take jobs. When the child-aid program was initiated, and for many years afterward, a fundamental purpose was to keep the mother at home with her children. This not only was considered good social policy but it fell in line with the desire during the Depression to discourage job-seeking by females and older persons so that there would be more employment opportunities for the traditional male breadwinner.

A Work Incentive (WIN) program, authorized by 1967 legislation and jointly administered by HEW and the Department of Labor, was designed to encourage AFDC mothers to seek work. This was to be done by allowing the mother to keep more of her monthly earnings without having her welfare check reduced.[17] Previously many states had reduced benefits dollar for dollar. Various services would be provided—education, training, work orientation, family planning services—to encourage job-

---

[17] She could keep the first $30 of her earnings plus one-third of the remainder after paying work expenses.

seeking. The program was not especially successful, partly because of the difficulty of providing child-care facilities.[18]

The program was revised by amendments adopted by Congress in December 1971 to create WIN II. The federal share of costs was increased and funds for child care were included; mothers were required to register for employment when their youngest child reached age six; and job placement was emphasized rather than training and orientation. Justification for the pressure on AFDC women to work was found in the fact that throughout the general population mothers had already entered the labor market in force, especially mothers of school-age children.[19] Among mothers in two-parent families whose children had reached school age, one-half were employed in 1973, compared with one-fourth 25 years earlier. Mothers in fatherless families with pre-school children were also working in large numbers. It is estimated that "at least 40 per cent of welfare mothers...work for some part of the year."[20]

Schedules Aligning Aid Benefits With Earnings

The application of so-called "benefit-loss rates"—that is, a schedule that determines how much a welfare benefit will be reduced because of earnings—introduces a new problem: how to develop a schedule that will sustain the incentive to work without giving the recipient an unfair advantage over a working person who does not receive welfare benefits. This problem is complicated still more when some of the welfare benefits are "in kind"—food stamps and Medicaid, for example—as well as cash. Benefit-loss rates apply to Social Security and SSI, public housing, AFDC, and food stamp programs. Other programs operate on an all-or-nothing basis.

For most of the life of the welfare system, the able-bodied male head of a two-parent family has not been considered a suitable recipient of the major aid system. Now that mothers are considered as able-bodied and suitable for employment as fathers, the discrepancy between their statuses in relation to welfare has lessened considerably. This trend has encouraged favorable consideration of a family allowance—a direct payment to maintain family income regardless of whether the father is present and in the job market or not. President Nixon in 1969 proposed a family allowance plan (FAP) as a substitute

---

[18] No federal funds were provided for acquisition of child-care facilities under the 1967 legislation. Robert Finch, the HEW Secretary, told the Ways and Means Committee in 1970 that "failure of day care in great part has contributed to the failure of the WIN program." See Sar Levitan, et al., *Work and Welfare Go Together* (1972), pp. 91-93. See also "Child Care," *E.R.R.*, 1972 Vol. II, pp. 441-458.

[19] See "Status of Women," *E.R.R.*, 1970 Vol. II, pp. 573-578.

[20] Subcommittee on Fiscal Policy of Joint Economic Committee of Congress, *Public Welfare and Work Incentives; Theory and Practice* (staff paper No. 14 of *Studies in Public Welfare* series), April 15, 1974, p. 3.

for welfare, but it was attacked as either too meager in benefits or too expensive. It failed to win congressional support and Nixon himself did not press for its enactment.[21] In his campaign for the presidency in 1972, Sen. George McGovern (D S.D.) proposed direct payments to individuals to sustain an income floor.

Food Stamps as Universal Form of Assistance

While the idea of a family allowance of some kind was ripening, but falling short of acceptance, the booming food stamp program was taking on some of the characteristics of a universal income-support plan. It is the only national welfare program that makes its benefits as readily available to families of able-bodied men as to others in need. Since food is a basic necessity, the opportunity to buy it at discount prices amounts to a cash benefit. Although use of the stamps is restricted to the purchase of domestically produced food products, it is obvious that savings on food purchases can be translated into greater purchasing power for other goods or services.

According to a congressional subcommittee staff paper: "The food stamp program now provides a larger income guarantee than the original (1969-70) family assistance plan level of $1,600 for a family of four, and offers a significant supplement to the working poor.... The extent to which it reduces poverty is unknown, however, since the census does not include the value of the food stamp bonus in official income statistics and poverty counts."[22] The program is illustrative of the difficulty of assessing the actual degree of poverty in the nation. The growth of "in-kind" benefits as a substitute for direct cash payments extends the proceeds from public welfare beyond that indicated by statistical analysis.[23]

President Ford, in a message to Congress on Oct. 21, 1975, proposed a National Food Stamp Reform Act aimed at stricter limitation on the number of beneficiaries. The administration bill would (1) limit eligibility for stamp purchase to those whose income is below the poverty line *(see footnote 3)*, (2) allow only a standard deduction of $100 a month ($125 for the elderly), (3) determine income on the basis of the previous three months (to prevent those employed on annual contracts, such as teachers, to become eligible for stamp purchases during vacation months), (4) establish a minimum age for qualification as a separate household, (5) require recipients to spend at least 30 per cent of their household income for stamps, (6) require able-bodied recipients to seek, accept and retain jobs, and (7) remove

---

[21] See Daniel P. Moynihan's *The Politics of a Guaranteed Income* (1973).

[22] *Public Welfare and Work Incentives*, p. 6.

[23] According to a study by a University of Virginia economics professor, Edgar K. Browning, the combination of cash and in-kind benefits has probably abolished poverty in the United States. See Browning's *Redistribution and the Welfare System* (1975), pp. 7-30.

the automatic eligibility for stamps that is granted to public assistance recipients. The President said his proposals would reduce the cost of the program by more than $1.2 billion a year.

Liberals have attacked the administration bill as too drastic a cutback, certain to cause suffering to needy families. "The food stamp program...needs some reform...[but] there is a difference between reform and dismemberment," Sen. Hubert H. Humphrey (D Minn.) testified on Oct. 7 during hearings conducted by the Senate Agriculture Committee. He was concerned that the bill would cast off low-income families headed by working parents that do not qualify for other forms of assistance. A substitute bill sponsored by Sens. Robert Dole (R Kan.) and McGovern would establish more liberal standards—maximum cash income for a family of four at $7,776, for example—and simplified administration. But reform of the food stamp program, Dole said, would be "merely...a stopgap on the road to comprehensive reform of the nation's social welfare system."

Ideas for Tax Credits and Family Allowances

One of the many pending bills on welfare reform may well be pointing the way toward the next major development in income support for low- and non-earning individuals and families. The bill, titled Tax Credits and Allowances Act of 1975, draws on the findings and recommendations of the Joint Economic Subcommittee on Fiscal Policy and is the product of the subcommittee's three-year study of the welfare problem *(see p. 129)*.

The proposed program would be in two parts: (1) tax relief for persons up to middle-income levels and (2) cash grants to the poor. The existing AFDC and food stamp programs would be scrapped. A tax credit of $225 per person would replace the personal exemption of $750 that now applies in the federal income tax system. Cash allowances would be paid to the poor to assure an income of $4,300 for a two-parent family of four, $3,-100 for a married couple, and $1,100 for a single adult. These cash allowances, called Allowances for Basic Living Expenses (ABLE), would be lowered by 50 cents per earned dollar. The subcommittee has estimated that 11.2 million families and individuals—34 million persons in all—would be eligible for grants and tax credits.

"The recommendations...would help lift the country from its economic recession, and would bring the welfare reward structure more nearly into accord with those activities that society values and the labor market rewards," said Mrs. Martha Griffiths (D Mich.), chairman of the subcommittee and chief instigator of the study, on releasing its findings Dec. 4, 1974.[24]

---

[24] The study was the culmination of Mrs.Griffiths' career in Congress. She did not seek re-election to the 94th Congress.

"...[It] would end the penalties on work, marriage, and family responsibility now found in many public welfare programs." President Ford, as a member of Congress, supported the FAP plan proposed by the Nixon administration. As President he may propose a family allowance or negative income tax plan of his own as a solution to the "welfare mess."

Bibliography

Books

Browning, Edgar K., *Redistribution and the Welfare System,* American Enterprise Institute, 1975.

Hazlitt, Henry, *The Conquest of Poverty,* Arlington House, 1973.

Komisar, Lucy, *Down and Out in the U.S.A.: A History of Social Welfare,* Franklin Watts, Inc., 1973.

Levitan, Sar, *The Great Society's Poor Law: A New Approach to Poverty,* Johns Hopkins University Press, 1969.

Levitan, Sar, et. al, *Work and Welfare Go Together,* Johns Hopkins University Press, 1972.

Schlesinger, Arthur Jr., *The Age of Roosevelt: The Coming of the New Deal,* Houghton Mifflin, 1958.

Steiner, Gilbert Y., *The State of Welfare,* The Brookings Institution, 1974.

Wilensky, Harold L., *The Welfare State and Equality,* University of California Press, 1975.

Articles

Glazer, Nathan, "Reform Work, Not Welfare," *Public Interest,* summer 1975.

Lampman, Robert J., "What does it do for the poor?—a new test for national policy," *Public Interest,* winter 1974.

Skolnik, Alfred M. and Sophie R. Dales, "Special Welfare Expenditures, Fiscal Year 1974," *Social Security Bulletin,* January 1975.

Taussig, A. Dale, "The Dual Welfare System," *Society,* January-February 1974.

Reports and Studies

"Current Operating Statistics," *Social Security Bulletin,* October 1975.

Editorial Research Reports: "Future of Social Programs," 1973 Vol. I, p. 249; "Redistribution of Income," 1972 Vol. II, p. 645; "Social Security Financing," 1972 Vol. II, p. 705; "Welfare Reforms," 1967 Vol. II, p. 928.

"Ford Plans Restructuring of Social Programs," *Congressional Quarterly Weekly Report,* July 26, 1975, p. 1613.

U.S. Congress, Joint Economic Committee, Subcommittee on Fiscal Policy, *Studies in Public Welfare* (staff papers Nos. 1-15, 1972-1974) and "Income Security for Americans: Recommendations of the Public Welfare Study," Dec. 5, 1974.

THE NEW IMMIGRATION

by

Sandra Stencel

Dec. 13
1 9 7 4

THE NEW IMMIGRATION

A NEW IMMIGRATION is taking place in America and is once again raising a national debate on an issue that has been so emotional and troublesome in other times. Major changes in the size and characteristics of America's immigrant population have occurred in the decade since the passage of the Immigration Act of 1965. The act marked a turning point in American immigration policy by ending the long-established and long-controversial policy of using national origin as a major criterion for admitting foreigners to this country. Moreover, American attitudes toward immigration also have changed in the intervening years.

The pro-immigration sentiment that was largely responsible for eliminating the inequities of the old system has been replaced in some quarters by concern about population growth, dwindling resources and the state of the economy. Does America really want—and can it afford—to extend the Statue of Liberty's invitation to the tired, the poor, the wretched refuse of the world, some Americans are asking? Is it time for this "nation of immigrants" to pull up the gangplank?[1] The current ambivalence toward immigration was evident in a recent speech by Attorney General William B. Saxbe. "With the manifold problems the nation faces—energy shortages, inflation, scarcity of some foodstuffs, rising unemployment—it is apparent that we are not a limitless horn of plenty," Saxbe told a local bar association meeting in Brownsville, Texas, on Oct. 30. "While we must help other nations all we can, we cannot let our own people suffer in the bargain."

Demands for more restrictive immigration policies come at a time when world food shortages and economic uncertainties abroad are making the United States increasingly attractive to foreigners. The volume of immigration already is increasing. In fiscal year 1965, a total of 296,697 immigrants were admitted into this country; by fiscal 1973, that number had grown to 400,063—a 34.8 per cent increase.[2] "Immigration is not about to

---

[1] Leslie Aldridge Westoff, "Should We Pull Up the Gangplank?" *The New York Times Magazine*, Sept. 16, 1973, p. 15.

[2] "1973 Annual Report" of the Immigration and Naturalization Service, p. 3.

decline" in the years ahead, according to Charles B. Keely, associate professor of sociology at Western Michigan University. "Rather, it would seem that the fiscal year 1973 may be the beginning of a new stage of immigration...."[3]

Shift in Origin of Newcomers Under 1965 Law

The most striking shift in the pattern of U.S. immigration in the last decade has been in the origins of the newcomers. Asia, southern and eastern Europe, Latin America and the Caribbean islands have replaced northern and western Europe as the primary sources of immigrants. There were six times as many Asian immigrants in 1973 as in 1965 and they accounted for one-third of the total. Meanwhile, immigration from northern and western Europe fell by two-thirds, as is shown below:

From	1965	1973	Change
Asia	20,683	124,160	Up 500%
Latin America	81,781	99,407	Up 22
Southern and Eastern Europe	40,106	68,322	Up 70
West Indies	37,583	64,765	Up 75
Northern Europe and Canada	111,645	33,499	Down 70
Africa	3,383	6,655	Up 97
Oceania	1,512	3,255	Up 115

These changes result from the 1965 Immigration Act, signed into law by President Johnson on Oct. 3, 1965, and fully operative July 1, 1968. It abolished the national origins system established by the Immigration Act of 1924, which assigned a nation's annual quota on the basis of the number of persons of that national origin already living in the United States in 1920. Consequently, large quotas were assigned to Britain, Ireland, Germany and the other northern and western European nations that had contributed heavily to immigration during the settlement of America. The 1924 law set no quotas for the western hemisphere but it barred the permanent entry of Asians.

In place of the old system, the 1965 law substitutes a limitation of 20,000 immigrants per country, with an overall limitation of 170,000 persons for the entire eastern hemisphere. Within this overall limitation, visas are allotted through a system of preferences. The new law gives a stronger preference to close relatives of U.S. citizens and resident aliens. Under the old law, 50 per cent of the quota was reserved for close relatives; under the 1965 law, 74 per cent. Remaining visas are reserved for (1) members of the professions, scientists and artists of exceptional ability, (2) skilled and unskilled workers in occupations for

---

[3] Charles B. Keely, "Immigration Composition and Population Policy," *Science*, Aug. 16, 1974, p. 590.

which labor is in short supply in the United States, and (3) refugees.

Another important change in immigration policy was the imposition of a limit for the first time on immigration from other countries in the western hemisphere. The Johnson administration opposed this limitation, but finally accepted it as the price of getting the national origins system repealed. The limitation was backed by the American Legion, the American Coalition of Patriotic Societies and others that feared the United States would suffer the effects of population growth in Latin America and the Caribbean. The visa preference system does not apply to the 120,000 immigrants allotted to the independent nations of the western hemisphere. Immigration from these countries is essentially on a first-come, first-served basis, with no individual-country limitation.

Concern Over 'Brain Drain' From Poor Nations

The newly arriving immigrants are very different from those of past generations. Unlike the impoverished and often illiterate laborers who once flocked to American shores, many of today's immigrants come from middle-class backgrounds and have professional or technical skills. "The old immigrants—our grandparents—left because nothing could be worse than what they had here," a teacher from the small Italian village of Mola told author Susan Jacoby. "The new immigrants leave because they already have something, but they hope for more than our own country can provide."[4]

From 1901 to 1930, a period of heavy immigration, only about 1.8 per cent of the immigrants had professional or technical skills; by 1973, nearly 10 per cent of the immigrants had such skills. About one-fifth of all Asian immigrants in 1973 and about one-fourth of the African immigrants were professional or technical workers. One reason for the increase in better-trained immigrants is the Labor Certification Program administered by the Labor Department. Under this program, would-be immigrants who are not refugees or close relatives of American citizens must obtain a certification from the department that their entry will not serve to lower the wages or working conditions of similarly employed Americans. The department also must certify that there are not sufficient workers already available in the United States to perform the type of labor the would-be immigrant is qualified to do.

Many of the professionally trained immigrants are employed in the health professions. Between 1969 and 1973, according to

---

[4] Susan Jacoby, "Immigrants: Roots," Part I, Report to the Alicia Patterson Foundation, Oct. 12, 1974.

official statistics, over 50,000 doctors and almost 40,000 nurses were admitted to the United States on permanent or temporary visas. The Association of American Medical Colleges reported that 46 per cent of all physicians licensed in 1972 were graduates of foreign medical schools. A large majority of the immigrant physicians—over 70 per cent, according to the National Science Foundation—came from India, the Philippines, Korea, Iran, Taiwan, Thailand, Pakistan and China.

"The net outflow of trained personnel from developing to developed countries is significant enough to justify international concern and to warrant the formulation and implementation of policies to reduce, if not to stop, this net outflow," U.N. Secretary General Kurt Waldheim declared in March 1974. Some observers are calling this migration the "new brain drain." The phrase first appeared in the 1960s, when thousands of scientists, engineers and physicians left Europe and the developing countries for better paying and more prestigious jobs in the United States.[5] The number of scientists and engineers migrating to this country has declined somewhat in recent years, primarily because of the certification requirements. However, the drain of medical talent, particularly from the developing countries, continues to rise.

In fact, the United States encourages this trend by its "failure to build sufficient medical schools to meet the growing demand for doctors in the nation's expanding health services" and by "the inefficient use of health manpower already available," according to a report prepared for the House Foreign Affairs Sub-committee on National Security Policy and Scientific Developments.[6] One indicator of the social costs of emigrating physicians, the report said, is doctor-to-population ratios. In the United States there are 1.7 doctors for every 1,000 inhabitants, compared with 1 to 10,000 in Africa; 1 to 5,700 in Asia; and 1 to 1,800 in Latin America. By importing so many foreign-trained physicians, scientists and engineers, the United States saved an estimated $1.7 billion in educational costs in 1971 and 1972. In effect, the report concluded, the brain drain makes the United States a recipient of "reverse foreign aid" from poor countries.

Efforts at Controlling the Influx of Illegal Aliens

The major concern of U.S. immigration officials at present is the flood of illegal aliens pouring into this country each year, especially from Latin America. No one knows for sure how many illegal immigrants are living in the United States. Estimates

---

[5] See "World Competition for Skilled Labor," *E.R.R.*, 1967 Vol. I, pp. 439-457.

[6] "Brain Drain: A Study of the Persistent Issue of International Scientific Mobility," September 1974. See also "Brain Drain Implications for U.S. Foreign Policy," *BioScience*, November 1974, p. 627.

Leading Sources of U.S. Immigrants

1965		1973	
1. Canada	38,327	1. Mexico	70,141
2. Mexico	37,969	2. Philippines	30,799
3. United Kingdom	27,358	3. Cuba	24,147
4. Germany	24,045	4. Korea	22,930
5. Cuba	19,760	5. Italy	22,151
6. Colombia	10,885	6. China and Taiwan	17,297
7. Italy	10,821	7. Dominican Republic	13,921
8. Dominican Republic	9,504	8. India	13,124
9. Poland	8,465	9. Greece	10,751
10. Argentina	6,124	10. Portugal	10,751
11. Ireland	5,463	11. United Kingdom	10,638
12. Ecuador	4,392	12. Jamaica	9,963
13. France	4,039	13. Canada	8,951
14. China and Taiwan	4,057	14. Yugoslavia	7,582
15. Haiti	3,609	15. Trinidad and Tobago	7,035

SOURCE: U.S. Immigration and Naturalization Service

usually range from four to seven million, but the commissioner of the Immigration and Naturalization Service, Leonard Chapman, has said it could be as high as 12 million, including perhaps as many as one million in New York City.[7] One clue to the dimensions of the illegal immigrant problem is the number of deportable aliens apprehended each year by the agency's Investigations and Border Patrol Divisions. In fiscal year 1965 the figure was 110,371; in fiscal 1973 it had grown to 655,968. Close to 800,000 illegal aliens were apprehended in fiscal 1974, according to Commissioner Chapman, who has predicted that the number will rise to one million in 1975.

The vast majority of illegal immigrants—including about 90 per cent of those apprehended in 1973—are Mexican nationals who manage to slip across the border undetected.[8] Sizable numbers of illegal immigrants come from British Honduras, the British West Indies, the Philippines, Greece and Italy. Some enter the country as tourists or students and then stay illegally after their visas officially expire. Others enter with forged documents or are smuggled in for high prices by organized smuggling rings. Some merchant seamen—mostly Chinese, Italians and Greeks—get in by deserting their ships while in U.S. ports. Some illegal immigrants manage to stay in the

[7] Figures cited in a speech to the New York Chamber of Commerce and Industry, Dec. 5, 1974.

[8] President Ford and Mexican President Echeverria, meeting in Nogales, Mexico, on Oct. 21, 1974, announced the establishment of a joint study team to investigate the problem of illegal immigration.

country by arranging fraudulent marriages with American citizens.

They come for the same reasons as legal immigrants: in search of jobs and a better way of life. Until recently, most persons who entered illegally were men hoping to earn some money and then return home to their families. Today many illegal entrants bring their families with them. Immigration officials also find that a growing number of unmarried women enter illegally, mainly to work as domestics for American families. The illegal immigrants are no longer concentrated in the fields and farms of the Southwest. Many of them have drifted away from rural "stoop labor" and into better paying city jobs. Today hundreds of thousands can be found washing dishes, waiting on tables or working in factories in Boston, New York, Philadelphia, Washington, Chicago, Los Angeles, Dallas and San Francisco.

Attorney General Saxbe told his Brownsville audience that illegal aliens "now hold at least 364,000 jobs in industry, nearly that many in agriculture, and some 300,000 in service trades" that might otherwise go to unemployed and low-income Americans or legally admitted aliens. In addition, Saxbe said, illegal immigrants "receive social services ranging from schools to welfare," send large amounts of money back to their native lands, pay little or no taxes on their incomes, and "mock our system of legal immigration."

Saxbe and Chapman support a bill in Congress to make it a crime to knowingly hire illegal aliens. The House passed the bill May 3 and it was sent to the Senate Judiciary Committee. No floor action is expected in 1974 but a spokesman for the chief sponsor, Rep. Peter W. Rodino Jr. (D N.J.), said Rodino planned to reintroduce the bill in the 94th Congress. A similar measure was enacted by the California legislature in 1971 after U.S. immigration officials found a number of illegal immigrants working in a food processing plant owned by Mrs. Romana Banuelos, President Nixon's appointee as Treasurer of the United States. However, in February 1972, one month before the law was to go into effect, an appellate court declared it unconstitutional on the ground that the federal government is preemptive in the field of immigration and naturalization.

Charges of Corruption in Immigration Service

The Rodino bill has been criticized by the American Civil Liberties Union and many Chicano leaders who fear that it would discourage employers from hiring anyone who even looks Mexican. Chicanos are concerned that a crackdown on illegal immigration might bring other hardships to the Mexican-American community. The ACLU has received numerous complaints concerning periodic sweeps of city streets, factories and public places by immigration agents looking for illegal aliens. Chicanos claim that immigration officials often harass brown-skinned people, regardless of their status in this country.

It has been charged that the current scope of illegal immigration is due, at least in part, to lax enforcement and official corruption. In May 1972, when Richard G. Kleindienst was Attorney General, he ordered an investigation of allegations that Border Patrol personnel were engaged in such activities as narcotics and alien smuggling, fraudulent sale of entry documents, prostitution, bribery and extortion. The following March, the House Subcommittee on Legal and Monetary Affairs opened an inquiry into the matter.

The subcommittee found evidence suggesting that the Justice Department had covered up evidence disclosed by its own investigation in order to protect high officials in the Immigration Service. After the cover-up charges were made public on June 11, 1974, by subcommittee counsel William G. Lawrence, Attorney General Saxbe and Commissioner Chapman ordered a new investigation. The findings of the new investigation concerning corruption and cover-up charges were due to be presented to a federal grand jury which was convened at San Diego on Nov. 25.

The Washington Post reported Dec. 10 that no indictments were recommended to the grand jury by a Justice Department investigator, who was identified as Alfred Hantman. He headed the original investigation ordered by Kleindienst in 1972, known as Operation Clean Sweep. Deputy Attorney General Laurence H. Silberman the same day denied before the congressional subcommittee what he described as "allegations of witnesses not being permitted to testify fully and openly...."

View of America's Immigrant Heritage

IMMIGRATION has been called "America's historic *raison d'être*...the most persistent and the most persuasive influence in her development."[9] The history of the United States has been molded by successive waves of immigrants. While other lands such as Argentina, Australia and Canada are also populated by immigrants, no other country has held the same attraction as

---

[9] Maldwyn Allen Jones, *American Immigration* (1960), p. 1.

the United States for so long, nor has any other country been settled by such a variety of peoples.

Migration restrictions by foreign countries limited the volume of newcomers during the first generation of American independence. It is officially estimated that 250,000 immigrants entered the United States between 1790 and 1820.[10] Britain and other European countries began to remove restrictions on emigration to the New World around 1815. Several reasons have been cited for the change, including large increases in population resulting from a decline in mortality rates. In addition, the industrial revolution and the growth of the factory system were destroying the old system of home manufacture and throwing countless artisans out of work.

"We are a nation of immigrants."

John F. Kennedy, *A Nation of Immigrants* (1958)*

Reorganization of the rural economy, moreover, was cutting loose from the soil a large part of the farm population. The dispossessed and the unemployed were encouraged to come to America by low steamship fares and by cheap railroad tickets to inland points; in many cases passage was paid by an American landholder or factory owner in need of low-cost labor. The opening of western lands to immigrants as well as to the native-born also afforded an inducement.

Though economic factors predominated in spurring emigration from Europe, political and religious discontent was also important. Awareness of the American guarantee of religious freedom and of the right of foreign-born citizens to occupy any political office except the presidency was widespread among political revolutionaries and religious non-conformists. The stage was thus set for a century-long exodus from the Old World to the New. Marcus L. Hansen described the vast movement as follows: "The years from the fall of Napoleon to the outbreak of the World War spanned exactly one hundred seasons of migration in which a great flood of humanity rolled westward across the Atlantic and swept over the waiting continent. To that flood

---

[10] U.S. Department of Commerce, *Historical Statistics of the United States, Colonial Times to 1957* (1960), p. 48. Although reporting of alien arrivals was required by an act of Congress in 1798, early records have not survived.

* Anti-Defamation League of B'nai B'rith pamphlet, republished after his death as a book.

every nation, every province, almost every neighborhood, contributed its stream."[11]

The first immigrants were mostly Irish and Scotch-Irish. From 50,000 in the 1820s, the influx of Irish quadrupled in the 1830s and went on to reach far larger proportions, particularly during Ireland's famine years of the 1840s; between 1840 and 1860, no fewer than 1.7 million Irish immigrants entered this country. The number of German arrivals rose similarly from a trickle in the 1820s to more than a million in the 10 years from 1846 through 1855—years marked by a series of crop failures in their homeland. And in the period of reaction that followed the revolutions of 1848 in various European nations, there was an exodus to America of a numerically small but prominent group of European intellectuals who were destined to make important contributions to their adopted country.

Immigration from England, Norway and Sweden, mounting after 1850, reached a peak in the 1880s. After 1890, immigration from the countries of southern and eastern Europe got under way. This new movement across the Atlantic reached tidal proportions from 1905 to 1914, when more than 10 million immigrants entered the United States, 65 per cent of them from Austria-Hungary, Italy and Russia. The only significant non-European immigration in the 19th century was from Canada, itself settled by Europeans, and from China. An outpouring of Chinese coolies, lured or dragooned to railroad construction in the West, was a major factor in bringing about the eventual exclusion of Orientals, although the actual number arriving between 1850 and 1890 was only 290,000.

Hostility to Newcomers and Rise of Nativism

The welcome extended the immigrants was tinged in many cases with misgivings about the political, religious and social problems the newcomers might bring. Differences in manners and mores dismayed many citizens. Differences of all kinds were prolonged by the tendency of most immigrant groups to form ethnic enclaves, the natural consequence of group migration and of the economic and geographic forces that determined settlement routes.

The differences became more than a matter of mere irritation in periods when unemployment spread and the presence of large numbers of persons of foreign birth stirred resentment in the competition for jobs. As immigrants flooded in, anti-foreign sentiment swelled. Fears raised by rapid growth of the Catholic population, by the aptitude of the Irish for politics and by the

---

[11] Marcus L. Hansen, *The Atlantic Migration, 1607-1860* (1940), p. 8.

alleged revolutionary tendencies of German immigrants culminated in the establishment in 1849 of the American, or Know-Nothing, political party. It engaged in propagating hostility to foreigners and Catholicism.[12]

The nativist-immigrant issue was obscured during the Civil War but reappeared later on the West Coast, where it was coupled with racial feelings over the influx of Chinese laborers. Riots and mob violence had been periodic for some years, but feeling ran so high in the 1870s that public pressure caused Congress, in 1882, to adopt the first important legislation restricting entry into the United States. The act suspended Chinese immigration for 10 years and forbade naturalization of the Chinese who were already here. The suspension was renewed in 1892 and made permanent in 1902.[13]

Congress in 1885 outlawed the practice of paying an immigrant's passage in return for his services, and in 1891 it moved to curb the widespread practice of advertising abroad for labor. Demands for more far-reaching restrictions gathered strength in succeeding years as immigration from the countries of northern and western Europe declined and immigration from southern and eastern Europe increased. The contemporary view was that these latter-day immigrants were unskilled, illiterate laborers unaccompanied by families. Demands arose for imposing a literacy test on new arrivals and bills to that end were passed by successive Congresses and vetoed in turn by Presidents Cleveland, Taft and Wilson. A literacy bill finally enacted over Wilson's veto in 1917 barred from admission, with certain exceptions, all aliens over 16 years of age who could not read English or some other language or dialect.

Congressional Action to Restrict Entry of Aliens

The great wave of immigration in the decade before World War I, and the beginning of another wave immediately after the war, led to the first quantitative limitations on immigration from Europe. Congress in 1921 assigned to each European country an annual quota equal to 3 per cent of the number of foreign-born of that nationality in the United States when the 1910 census was taken. The overall quota came to 357,000. Britain and Ireland together were allowed the most, 77,000, followed by Germany, 68,000; Italy, 42,000; Russia, 34,000; and Poland, 26,000.

Loopholes in the law let in far more than Congress had intended and led to a new statute in 1924. It set up two systems of

---

[12] See John Higham's *Strangers in the Land: Patterns of American Nativism 1860-1925* (1963), pp. 3-11.

[13] See "Oriental Exclusion," *E.R.R.*, 1943 Vol. I, pp. 359-374.

American Immigration, 1821-1970

Years	Numbers	Years	Numbers
1821-1830	143,439	1901-1910	8,795,386
1831-1840	599,125	1911-1920	5,735,811
1841-1850	1,713,251	1921-1930	4,107,209
1851-1860	2,598,214	1931-1940	528,431
1861-1870	2,314,824	1941-1950	1,035,039
1871-1880	2,812,191	1951-1960	2,515,479
1881-1890	5,246,613	1961-1970	3,321,677
1891-1900	3,687,564		

SOURCE: U.S. Immigration and Naturalization Service

determining quotas. The first, to be effective for three years, cut the annual country quotas from 3 to 2 per cent and based the computation on the 1890 instead of the 1910 census, thus drastically cutting down the numbers admissible from southern and eastern Europe. Of the total quota of 165,000 a year for Europe, 85 per cent would come from northern and western Europe. The second, and permanent, method of reckoning quotas, authorized to take effect in 1927 but actually deferred to 1929, was designed to preserve the nation's existing ethnic composition. It divided an annual quota of 150,000 among the various countries of Europe in the same way that the population of the United States in 1920 was divided among groups whose family origin stemmed from those countries.

The national origins system required little change in the small quotas assigned to countries of southern and eastern Europe, but it entailed substantial reductions in the German, Irish and Scandinavian quotas and a large increase for the British. Their quota of 66,000 was larger by 40,000 than Germany's quota of 26,000 which was the next largest. The effect was to cut actual immigration far below the volume authorized by the law, because Britain never filled its quota. From 1931 until the end of World War II, annual quota immigration never reached 100,000.

Confronted after World War II by the need to provide for a million refugees from Communist-dominated eastern Europe, Congress in 1948 passed the Displaced Persons Act to admit almost 400,000 refugees in addition to annual quota immigration. This led to demands for a general overhaul of immigration laws. The ensuing debate revealed a sharp division of opinion between persons who wished to do away with the national origins system, and otherwise liberalize immigration policy, and persons intent on retaining a restrictive policy. Passage of the Immigration and Nationality Act of 1952, over

President Truman's veto, represented a victory for the restrictionists.

The 1952 law, better known as the McCarran-Walter Act,[14] retained the system of quotas based on national origin and added token quotas for Asian countries and for new nations coming into existence. To limit overall immigration, the act continued to prohibit the transfer of unused quotas from one country to another and the carryover of unused quotas from one year to the next. Provisions for screening non-immigrant aliens planning to visit the United States, as well as would-be immigrants, were adopted. Grounds for excluding aliens were broadened, and fingerprinting of all aliens entering the country was required; grounds for deporting aliens and denaturalizing citizens also were broadened.

Survival of Ethnic Identity Despite Melting Pot

"America is God's Crucible, the great Melting Pot where all the races of Europe are melting and re-forming." In those words playwright Israel Zangwill, a British-born Jew, described his vision of America—a country where diverse ethnic and religious groups soon blended into a homogeneous mass. The myth of the "melting pot" had a prominent place in American thought even before Zangwill coined the phrase in 1908. French-American author Michael Guillaume Jean de Crèvecoeur, in his *Letters from an American Farmer*, wrote in 1782 that in the United States "individuals of all nations are melted into a new race of men." Over a century later American school children, the children and grandchildren of immigrants, often took part in symbolic rites of assimilation by marching through a cardboard melting pot, from which they emerged waving American flags.

Even then some Americans did not accept the melting pot philosophy. In an influential series of articles in *The Nation* magazine in 1915, philosopher Horace M. Kallen denied that it was possible or desirable for the immigrant groups to lose their identity and he argued that American culture had much to gain by permitting each of them to develop its own particular tendencies.[15] Advocates of cultural pluralism continued to speak out throughout the 20th century, but it was not until the 1960s that ethnicity emerged as a powerful social and political force. The rediscovery of America's ethnic heritage has been described by historian Oscar Handlin:

> The tendency was most visible and most dramatic among disadvantaged Americans—blacks, Chicanos, and Puerto Ricans who thought they needed an ethnic explanation of their situation.

---

[14] For its co-authors, Sen. Pat McCarran (D Nev.) and Rep. Francis E. Walter (D Pa.).

[15] Oscar Handlin (ed.), *Immigration as a Factor in American History* (1959), pp. 153-155.

But other elements in the population...also felt a revival of sentiments linking them to their ethnic origins.

There now seemed an advantage to identification, just as earlier there had been an advantage to assimilation. In part the advantage was economic. Formerly, preferences had gone to individuals who conformed to a favored type in dress, speech, manners and family connections. Now the term, WASP [White Anglo-Saxon Protestant], bore a slightly negative connotation....

But the source of the pull toward ethnicity was not simply economic in origin. All the cultural and social pressures of life in the 1960s also generated an inner desire for the security that such identifications brought. Therefore they huddled together, narrowed in upon one another, seeking in the nest of the familiar the security lacking in the wide open spaces.[16]

Another explanation for the ethnic revival was offered by sociologists Nathan Glazer and Daniel P. Moynihan. They suggested that ethnic groups were not only a source of individual identity, but had become interest groups by which persons sought to defend or advance their positions in society.[17]

Much criticized as bigots and racists, white ethnics saw themselves as forgotten people, trapped between poor blacks and Spanish-Americans who were eligible for public housing, medical benefits, job training and food stamps, and the WASPS who were in control of the power structure. Most ethnics did not contend that they were worse off than other minorities, but they maintained that they, too, had been excluded from positions of power.[18]

Future Role of Ethnicity in America

ETHNIC MILITANCY seems to have subsided recently, or at least the press is paying less attention to it. But the public's interest in ethnic heritage apparently has not dimmed. Historians, sociologists, anthropologists and other social scientists are turning out countless books and articles on the origin and development of ethnic institutions and on the contributions of immigrants to the arts, politics, and labor organizations. The Ford and Rockefeller Foundations are spending millions of dollars to support research in ethnic studies and to aid action programs in ethnic communities. The National Center for Urban Ethnic Affairs, set up in 1969 by Monsignor Geno C. Baroni in Wash-

---

[16] Oscar Handlin, *The Uprooted*, 2nd edition (1973), p. 276.

[17] Nathan Glazer and Daniel P. Moynihan, *Beyond the Melting Pot* (1963). See also their article "Why Ethnicity?" in *Commentary*, October 1974, pp. 33-39.

[18] See "Ethnic America," *E.R.R.*, 1971 Vol. I, pp. 45-64.

ington, D.C., has community organizers in more than 35 cities in the Northeast and Midwest. The Center for Immigration Studies of the University of Minnesota is collecting material for its Immigrant Archives to aid and encourage research into the contributions of the "forgotten immigrants" from eastern, southern and central Europe, and the Middle East.

Ethnic Studies Programs and Bilingual Education

Evidence of public acceptance of the new ethnicity can be seen in the number of ethnic studies offered by colleges and public schools. Federal support for such programs was obtained in the Ethnic Heritage Studies Program Act, signed into law on June 23, 1972, as part of the Omnibus Higher Education Amendments of 1972 and subsequently extended through fiscal year 1978. During the program's first year of operation, from mid-1973 to mid-1974, 42 grants totaling almost $2.4 million were awarded. The legislation, as stated in its preamble, is "...to provide assistance designed to afford to students opportunities to learn about the nature of their own cultural heritage, and to study the contributions of...other ethnic groups in the nation."

Since 1968 Congress has authorized federal funds for bilingual educational programs.[19] It is estimated that five million children enrolled in the nation's public schools have English language deficiencies, according to the Department of Health, Education, and Welfare. These include children whose heritage is Mexican, Puerto Rican, Cuban, Portuguese, Chinese, Japanese, Filipino, Korean and American Indian. The plight of the language-minority child was described by the Senate Select Committee on Equal Educational Opportunity in its final report, "Toward Equal Educational Opportunity," issued on Dec. 31, 1972:

> Like black and poor white children he may be isolated in a rural slum or urban ghetto....But when he arrives at school he faces a special disadvantage, for his language and culture are different, and often neither is valued or understood by those who teach him and run his school. His language is considered alien, his culture unimportant, and his manner unusual....

> The language-minority child is tested; the test he takes was designed for middle-class, English-speaking "Anglo" children; he fails or does poorly; he is then tracked into a class with slow learners; he sees himself as inferior.... What these conditions add up to is a conscious or unconscious policy of linguistic and cultural exclusion and alienation.

Public interest in bilingual education has increased in the past year in light of a Supreme Court ruling on Jan. 21, 1974, in the

---

[19] The Bilingual Education Act was enacted in 1967 as Title VII of the Elementary and Secondary Education Act.

case of Lau *v.* Nichols. In a unanimous decision, the Court held that the San Francisco school system illegally discriminated against some 1,800 Chinese-American students by failing to help them surmount the language handicap, thereby denying them "a meaningful opportunity to participate in the public educational program." The school district's failure to take positive action to help students who are not fluent in English, the Court said, violated Section 601 of the Civil Rights Act of 1964, which bans discrimination "on the ground of race, color or national origin" in programs receiving financial assistance.

Possible Disadvantages of Emphasis on Diversity

Bilingual education, according to Sen. Alan Cranston (D Calif.), "clearly rejects the idea that the prime objective of the school is to wipe out all the differences in style, heritage, and language background.... This is the route that schooling in America has traveled historically...and it reflects an anti-minority tradition in American public education that is only now beginning to change."[20] Such attacks on public education's role in the assimilation of immigrant children has provoked a reaction. "I believe the 'Americanization' of the immigrant was a great achievement, an almost unique and unparalleled achievement despite its harshness and arrogance," Nathan Glazer wrote recently. "I am not sure that the immigrants who came to this country willingly, to work and to become citizens of a new land, were deprived when they gave up an old language for English, old cultures for a new emerging culture, old allegiances for a new allegiance."[21]

Stephen S. Rosenfeld, in a signed editorial page column in *The Washington Post*, expressed the fear that bilingual education "might make kids even less competent and less motivated to deal in a competitive English-speaking society."[22] Howard Phillips, writing in the conservative weekly *Human Events*, suggested that bilingualism was "a semantically appealing cover slogan for liberal activists who wish to emphasize those things which divide Americans...rather than those which unite us."[23]

Opponents of bilingual education are not the only ones asking whether the new ethnicity is weakening the common American glue and aggravating ethnic tensions and differences. William S. Bernard, director of the Center for Migration Studies of Brooklyn College and a member of the American Immigration and Citizenship Conference, wrote: "Too much stress on ethnici-

---

[20] Quoted in *The Washington Post*, Sept. 22, 1974.
[21] Nathan Glazer, "Ethnicity and the Schools," *Commentary*, September 1974, p. 59.
[22] *The Washington Post*, Sept. 27, 1974.
[23] Howard Phillips, "Bilingualism Masks Leftist Drive for Cultural Separatism," *Human Events*, Sept. 28, 1974, p. 8.

ty can be a drawback if it is unselective and dogmatic, retarding the adjustments that are normal and necessary to integration. Ethnic pride carried to the point of extreme and emotional ethnocentrism can assert itself in a dislike, a contempt, even a hatred for people of other ethnic backgrounds." "On the other hand," Bernard went on to say, "the virtues of ethnicity are also abundant. One can learn more easily from people of one's own ethnic background, who can translate the new conditions, both psychologically and linguistically."[24]

Proposals for Restricting Future Immigration

As America struggles to achieve a balance between the melting pot philosophy and the attractions of cultural pluralism, the question arises: Should future immigration to the United States be curbed? There already are signs that the country is moving in this direction. The board of directors of the organization Zero Population Growth, in April 1974, adopted the position that "legal immigration should be reduced to a level approximating emigration." This would reduce immigration to one-tenth of its current level since only about 40,000 U.S. citizens leave the country each year.

A task force of the Association of American Medical Colleges has recommended a major reduction in the number of foreign medical school graduates allowed to practice in the United States[25] and the State Department has issued new guidelines that make it harder for foreign students to obtain visas to attend American colleges. The State Department's action was prompted, in part, by concern about foreign students who stay illegally after their visas expire. It is estimated that 150,000 foreign nationals now attend American colleges and universities. The Immigration Service also has made it more difficult for foreign students to get work permits for summer jobs.

Canada, which opened its doors wide for years, recently has moved to tighten its immigration policies. The Canadian Minister of Manpower and Immigration, Robert Andras, announced in October that foreigners who want to come to Canada in the future, in most cases, will have to have jobs waiting for them or be willing to go to remote areas where their skills are needed. "Immigrants are applying and arriving in increasing numbers at a time when employment levels may well be uncertain, when housing is scarce and expensive, and many social services are strained to a critical point," Andras told the House of

[24] William S. Bernard, "The Ethnic Factor in the Integration of Immigrants," in *The New Immigration and the New Ethnicity*, edited by William S. Bernard and Judith Herman (pamphlet of the American Immigration and Citizenship Conference, 1974), p. 3.

[25] Association of American Medical Colleges, "Graduates of Foreign Medical Schools in the United States: A Challenge to Medical Education," 1974.

Immigrants and The Schools

"Once upon a time there was a great nation which became great because of its public schools. That is the American school legend.... The public school system, it is generally claimed, built American democracy. It took the backward poor, the ragged, ill-prepared ethnic minorities who crowded into the cities, educated and Americanized them, molded them into the homogeneous productive middle class that is America's strength and pride.

"But that story is simply not true.... The rate of school failure among the urban poor, in fact, has been consistently high since before 1900. The truth is that the immigrant children dropped out in great numbers—to fall back on the customs and skills their families brought with them to America. It was in spite of, and not because of, compulsory public education that some eventually made their way."

—Colin Greer, *The Great School Legend: A Revisionist Interpretation of American Public Education* (1972)

Commons on Oct. 22. "These strains are being felt particularly in our three major cities, where more than one-half of the immigrants who arrived this year will settle."

Arguments for more restrictive immigration policies in the United States also center on the worsening economic situation and the need to control growth. Advocates of zero population growth are among the most vocal supporters of limiting immigration further. Leslie Aldridge Westoff calls immigration "the last frontier of population growth." Opponents of this position argue that it has yet to be demonstrated that immigration is a major contributor to whatever population problem the United States has.

No-growth advocates often cite the findings of the Commission on Population Growth and the American Future to justify their position.[26] Actually there was a division of opinion on the immigration question. Some commission members felt that immigration should be decreased gradually, about 10 per cent a year for five years. The majority, however, thought that the present level of immigration should be maintained "because of the humanitarian aspects; because of the contribution which immigrants have made and continue to make to our society; and because of the importance of the role of the United States in international migration." The commission asked that migration policy be reviewed periodically to reflect demographic conditions and other considerations. When the 1965 law was passed, population control and the quality of life hardly entered the debate.

---

[26] Commission on Population Growth and the American Future, *Population and the American Future* (1972). John D. Rockefeller III was chairman.

Selected Bibliography

Books

Glazer, Nathan, and Daniel Patrick Moynihan, *Beyond the Melting Pot*, The MIT Press and Harvard University Press, 1963.

Handlin, Oscar, ed., *Immigration As A Factor in American History*, Prentice-Hall, 1959.

—*The Uprooted*, 2nd edition, Little, Brown and Co., 1973.

Hansen, Marcus Lee, *The Atlantic Migration, 1607-1860*, Harper & Row, 1940.

Higham, John, *Strangers in the Land: Patterns of American Nativism 1860-1925*, Atheneum, 1967.

Jones, Maldwyn Allen, *American Immigration*, The University of Chicago Press, 1960.

Novak, Michael, *The Rise of the Unmeltable Ethnics: Politics and Culture in the Seventies*, Macmillan, 1972.

Articles

Day, Mark, "Illegal Immigrants: A View From the Barrio," *The Progressive*, February 1974.

Glazer, Nathan, "Ethnicity and the Schools," *Commentary*, September 1974.

—and Daniel P. Moynihan, "Why Ethnicity?" *Commentary*, October 1974.

Keely, Charles B., "Immigration Composition and Population Policy," *Science*, Aug. 16, 1974.

Novak, Michael, "The New Ethnicity," *The Center Magazine*, July-August 1974.

Steinman, Clay, "Scapegoats of Unemployment," *The Nation*, April 17, 1972.

Westoff, Leslie Aldridge, "Should We Pull Up the Gangplank?" *The New York Times Magazine*, Sept. 16, 1973.

"Brain Drain Implications for U.S. Foreign Policy," *BioScience*, November 1974.

Reports and Studies

Association of American Medical Colleges, "Graduates of Foreign Medical Schools in the United States: A Challenge to Medical Education," 1974.

Bernard, William S., and Judith Herman, eds., "The New Immigration and The New Ethnicity," American Immigration and Citizenship Conference, 1974.

Editorial Research Reports, "Ethnic America," 1971 Vol. I, p. 45; "Immigration Policy," 1957 Vol. I, p. 85; "Immigration Policy Revision," 1964 Vol. I, p. 101; "Oriental Exclusion," 1943 Vol. I, p. 359; and "World Competition for Skilled Labor," 1967 Vol. I, p. 439.

House Subcommittee on National Security Policy and Scientific Development, "Brain Drain: A Study of the Persistent Issue of International Scientific Mobility," September 1974.

U.S. Immigration and Naturalization Service, "1973 Annual Report."

Volunteer Army

by

David Boorstin

June 20
1 9 7 5

VOLUNTEER ARMY

T HE PRESIDENT'S AUTHORITY to induct young men into the armed forces expired at midnight on June 30, 1973. In fact, conscription had ended almost six months earlier, as Secretary of Defense Melvin R. Laird confirmed on Jan. 27 when he announced, "the armed forces henceforth will depend exclusively on volunteer soldiers, sailors, airmen and marines. The use of the draft has ended." One of the most divisive national controversies appeared to end with it. Yet even as anxiety over the draft disappeared, there were doubts about the feasibility—and the desirability—of returning to an all-volunteer force.

Two years later, many of these doubts have been allayed. After a slow beginning in 1973, the armed forces met and even exceeded their enlistment goals for 1974 and the first four months of 1975. The Army, which had been the most reliant on draftees and the focus for fears about the all-volunteer concept, has actually had more recruits than it can use. Even Rep. F. Edward Hébert (D La.), former chairman of the House Armed Services Committee, who had always insisted that "the only way to get an all-volunteer army is to draft it," has changed his mind.

But Hébert and others fear that the current recruiting success may be largely attributable to the nation's economic troubles. Young men may be signing up to escape unemployment. A report prepared by the Brookings Institution for the Senate Armed Services Committee in June 1973 noted: "Possibly one of the least certain—and most important—elements affecting the maintenance of a volunteer force is the impact of unemployment on an individual's inclination to volunteer." The report suggested that the two did not appear to have a strong relation, pointing out that in 1970 those states with high unemployment did not necessarily have a high volunteer rate.[1] Others feel that the correlation between unemployment and enlistment is reasonably well established.[2]

[1] Martin Binkin and John D. Johnston, "All-Volunteer Armed Forces: Progress, Problems, and Prospects," June 1, 1973, pp. 43-44.
[2] For example, David B. Cortright, writing in *The Progressive*, September 1973, on "The Military Recruitment Racket," quoted a 1967 study done for the Pentagon by two economists who found that "a given percentage change in the unemployment rate for male youth was associated with a similar percentage change in Army enlistment rate."

However, there is no conclusive evidence for either point of view. Martin Binkin, co-author of the Brookings report, told Editorial Research Reports that he expects the unemployment-enlistment issue to be raised again when the economy returns to "full" employment. Then the experience of the last two and a half years would be especially useful to a nation called on to choose among the options available to increase or maintain the quantity and quality of enlisted personnel: Increased advertising, pay, fringe benefits, or even a return to the inactive but still extant Selective Service System *(see box)*.

The American attempt to maintain a peacetime volunteer force of 2.1 million men and women is unprecedented in any country's history. It means enlisting one out of every three qualified and available men under 23. Even if the volunteer force can be maintained, there are those who doubt that it is in the nation's best interests. Questions of social and economic justice are involved, as well as politics, foreign policy and military strategy. The ramifications of the volunteer Army extend far beyond the recruiting offices and the barracks.

Questions of Quality Among the Military Enlistees

The success of the return to a volunteer Army is being measured by the quality as well as by the number of new recruits. The proposed strength for all the armed forces is presented by the President in the annual federal budget, and authorized by Congress. Standards of quality are largely set, and measured, by the Army itself. "Quality is measured in terms of four factors: aptitude for the service, motivation, moral background and physical condition," Secretary of the Army

---

Selective Service Lives

Despite the switch to an all-volunteer force, the Selective Service System is alive and well in Washington and in local draft boards throughout the United States. It still registers some two million 18-year-olds annually, issues them draft cards, and holds lotteries matching birth dates to call-up numbers. The idea is to have a pool of men ready for the armed forces to draw upon, should an emergency force Congress to reinstate the draft.

Federal prosecutors have obtained thousands of indictments for Selective Service Law violations since the advent of the all-volunteer Army. Failure to register for the draft is the most common charge, and most of those convicted are fined and put on probation. Deliberate intent not to register is the cause of most prosecutions, and this can be avoided by enlisting. Thus some men may be forced to join the Army to avoid a felony conviction, even though they cannot be drafted.

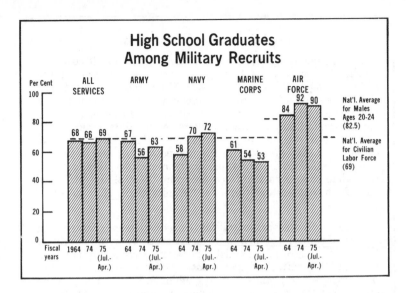

High School Graduates Among Military Recruits

Howard H. Callaway told Congress earlier this year. "Aptitude for the service is largely, though by no means completely, a function of education and mental category."[3]

On the basis of testing, volunteers are grouped into five mental categories. About 9 per cent of the U.S. population falls into the lowest group, Category V. Persons in this group are disqualified from military service by law. Enlistees in the next lowest category (IV) are considered by the services to require more training and present greater disciplinary problems than those in higher groups. They comprised 15 per cent of all enlistees in 1964 (20 per cent in the Army), in contrast to about 7 per cent now. The percentage of enlistees in Category III (average) has been increasing, although the percentage in I and II (above average) has decreased slightly.

High school graduates are regarded by manpower planners as better prospective soldiers. They account for fewer disciplinary problems and premature discharges. About 69 per cent of the new enlistees in the armed forces since mid-1974 have been high school graduates, the same percentage as in America's civilian labor force[4] *(see graph above)*. But they are distributed unevenly among the armed forces. High school graduates are more likely to be found in the Air Force and Navy than in the Army and Marine Corps. The Army's objectives in fiscal year 1976, as listed by Secretary Callaway, include plans to:

Increase the proportion of high school graduates to 80 per cent and the college-trained (one year or more of college) to 10 per cent.

---

[3] Statement to the House Committee on Armed Services, Feb. 26, 1975, p. 14.

[4] However, 82.5 per cent of the 20-24 year-old males in the labor force are high school graduates, according to the Bureau of Labor Statistics.

How Much Does VOLAR Cost?

One argument against the volunteer force is that it costs too much. Manpower costs have grown from 43 per cent of the defense budget in fiscal year 1964 to 55 per cent at present. The Department of Defense argues that ending the draft has had little to do with higher manpower costs. It has said that increases in pay for the military's civilian workers and in military retirement pay—both unrelated to the all-volunteer program—have accounted for three-quarters of the manpower cost increases. The rise in military pay, accounting for the remainder, is only partly related to the voluntary force program. Most of the increases stem from congressional action in 1967, six years before the draft ended.

Since pay increases for military careerists were granted as a matter of equity, a return to the draft probably would not affect them. If the pay of junior enlisted personnel were reduced under a return to the draft, the Department of Defense calculates, the annual savings might range from $1.5 billion to $3 billion, depending on whether Congress used the federal minimum wage or federal poverty level as a guideline for establishing reduced pay levels. Such a reduction would trim the manpower share of the defense budget only one or two percentage points. If current pay levels were maintained, savings in recruiting costs, bonuses and other special expenses would amount to only about $325 million and would have no appreciable effect on the manpower share of the budget.

The figures are not universally accepted. The federal Defense Manpower Commission, under the chairmanship of former Selective Service Director Curtis Tarr, is studying military manpower expenses and is due to report to Congress in 1976. A recent study by Martin Binkin of the Brookings Institution, *The Military Pay Muddle*, contends that the U.S. military pay system is a "costly anachronism" that causes the country to spend "more than is necessary to field its military forces."

Raise from 53 per cent to 60 per cent the share of those entering the Army from the top half of the population, according to mental-category ranking, while cutting the share in the lowest acceptable category to 15 per cent or less.

However, attempts to raise the mental and educational level of volunteers pose a difficult question: how much "quality" do the services really require? This is especially important in considering incentive payments for certain groups, because such bonuses could be buying more quality than is necessary.

Under a law enacted May 10, 1974, the armed forces are authorized to pay bonuses to men and women who enlist for at least four years and accept jobs that are termed critical. The Army, for example, currently designates 11 job skills as being critical: four, including service in hard-to-fill infantry and armored divisions, qualify the enlistee for a $2,500 bonus; the other seven, including service in artillery, engineer and missile units, qualify the enlistee for $1,500.[5] Similarly, the Selective Reenlistment Bonus (SRB) is being used to keep in service the GIs who have critical skills. Those with 21 months to 10 years of service qualify for up to $15,000 (currently $12,000 in the Army), depending on their base pay, the additional length of time they choose to serve, and the current "multiplier" value attached to a particular skill.

Multipliers are periodically reviewed; for example, an infantryman in the early 1970s was given the top multiplier of five but is now accorded a two, while a Hawk missile mechanic remains a top-priority five. These reviews can create enlistment problems. The recruit who signs up for a much-needed job specialty in the hope of earning a generous SRB when he reenlists, may find his skill no longer critically needed—nor financially rewarded—when the time comes for him to "re-up."

Both the Enlistment and Selective Reenlistment bonuses have been scaled down lately as the number of critical skill categories has been reduced. Enlistment bonuses are expected to cost the Army about $55 million in fiscal 1976, down from about $59 million in fiscal 1975. SRB costs are expected to remain at the current annual rate of $28 million. These reenlistment bonuses are credited, along with civilian unemployment, with a rise in Army reenlistment rates,[6] as is shown below:

	1973 Reenlistments	1974 Reenlistments
Among first-termers	16%	33%
Among career personnel	30	41

Each reenlistment reduces the need for a new recruit, diminishes training and recruiting costs, and contributes to maintaining trained strength at desired levels. Reenlistments also fill the Army's "middle years" and improve its content of career personnel—those with more than three years of service.

Concern Over Army's Social and Racial Makeup

In military terms, the quality of the Army is ultimately measured by its combat-readiness. In this respect, the Army portrays the volunteer force as a success. In its year-end report for 1974, the Department of the Army stated: "The readiness of our total force, the Active Army, National Guard, and the Army

---

[5] The statutory limit for enlistment bonuses is $3,000, but the Secretary of Defense has limited bonuses to $2,500. In addition to the requirement that recruits sign up for at least four years, one year longer than the minimum period of service, the Army also restricts bonuses to high school graduates in mental categories I, II or III.

[6] "The Army 1974: Year-End Report," Department of the Army, 1975, p. II-5.

Reserve, is significantly improved. At the time the last soldier was drafted in 1972, just four of the Army's Active divisions were considered combat-ready. By the end of 1973, 10 divisions were considered ready. Today, all 13 Active Army divisions are combat-ready."

The standards for judging the armed forces in a democratic society include their makeup and character as well as their proficiency at military tasks. "What we seek, and need, are quality soldiers—men and women—who are representative of the overall population," Secretary Callaway has said. "Ideally, we would like to have at least one person from every block in every city, one from every rural delivery route, and one from every street in every small town. Our obligation to the American people is to strive to field an Army which is both representative of them and acceptable to them."[7] President Ford, in a speech honoring the Army's 200th anniversary on June 14, called it "an Army of winners...truly representative of the American people."

Fear that the volunteer force would draw too many black and low-income youths was one of the earliest and strongest impediments to the volunteer concept. This was especially true when American soldiers were fighting and dying in Vietnam. Sen. Edward M. Kennedy (D Mass.) said during an extensive Senate debate on the subject on Aug. 25, 1970: "It is inequitable to permit the risks of battle to fall only on those less affluent Americans who are induced to join the Army by a pay raise...it is unwise to insulate from the horrors of war middle- and upper-class Americans who might lead the protest against senseless foreign adventures." Kennedy and others came to support the volunteer army concept when America's military involvement in Vietnam diminished, but the concern remained, and the Senate Armed Services Committee, in May 1974, asked the Pentagon for a report on population representation in the volunteer force.

The findings of the Pentagon report, submitted Dec. 17, were that in fiscal year 1974 the representation of new enlistees and the active force as a whole was close to that of the general population—with the exception of minority representation.

> Black personnel [the report stated] constituted about 21 per cent of new enlistees compared to 13 per cent in the general population. The black enlisted component of the force as a whole is 16 per cent in the enlisted ranks and 14 per cent when officers are included.... Black representation is comparable to certain related occupational fields in the civilian sector (e.g., 19 per cent for service workers and 20 per cent for non-farm laborers).

Geographically, the report continued, the number of new enlistees from each state tends to be proportional to the youth

---

[7] Statement before the House Committee on Armed Services, Feb. 26, 1975, p. 15.

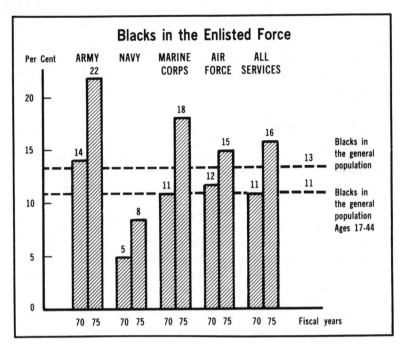

Blacks in the Enlisted Force

Per Cent ARMY NAVY MARINE AIR ALL
22 CORPS FORCE SERVICES

Blacks in the general population: 13

Blacks in the general population Ages 17-44: 11

70 75 70 75 70 75 70 75 70 75 Fiscal years

population in that state. However, on a regional basis, the northern and northeastern states supply relatively fewer volunteers and the southern and southeastern states relatively more in terms of population. As for the economic background of the recruits, the information—though "limited"—"indicates that recruits for the most part come from middle-income families. Few come from families where incomes are either high or very low."

The significance of these figures in a peacetime army remains problematic. The overrepresentation of blacks is seen as a threat by some and as evidence of economic and social injustice by others. Lt. Gen. Harold G. Moore, the Army's Deputy Chief of Staff for Personnel, sees it as "a positive reflection of that group's awareness of opportunities available in the Army."[8]

Political Implications of All-Professional Army

Whatever the social makeup of today's armed forces, their professional, volunteer nature has profound implications. Without the "citizen-soldier" to provide a civilian leavening, it has been argued, America's massive standing defense force could become isolated, even alienated, from those it has sworn to defend. At the extreme, this is seen as the threat that a military caste might develop as a repressive political force. A retired Army officer has suggested, "The Army could become increasingly involved in settling domestic disputes between poor,

---

[8] Statement before the Senate Subcommittee on Defense Appropriations, March 13, 1975.

disenfranchised black and white Americans and the forces of government supported by some middle- and upper-class citizens." In such a situation, no conspiratorial "coup mentality" would be necessary for the military to subvert civilian government.[9]

Of more immediate concern, however, is the possibility that the all-volunteer force might remove a potent inhibition on any decision to wage war. "It is conceivable that casualties suffered by a volunteer force would be more acceptable to the public as a whole than would casualties suffered by a drafted force...," two West Point graduates, Lt. Cols. Frederic J. Brown and Zeb B. Bradford Jr., have written.[10] On the other hand, they said, "A large and steady flow of replacements is a prerequisite for a sustained war on any significant scale" and "we should not assume that we can attract sufficient volunteers in wartime to replace large losses even in a popular war." Thus, while adventurism might conceivably be encouraged, the decision to engage in an extended conflict—such as the war in Vietnam—would be more difficult to make, since it would require legislative action to reinstitute the draft or mobilize the reserves.

Experience With Volunteer Forces

THE UNITED STATES relied on volunteers to win its War of Independence and, except for a few intervals during the next two centuries, continued to rely on them. The draft is associated with the need for massive armies, a relatively recent development in history. Mass warfare came to the United States in the Civil War, and both sides resorted to conscription when it became apparent that the volunteer system was incapable of furnishing enough troops. In March 1863, two years after the war began, Congress enacted the nation's first conscription law. It was designed to stimulate the flow of Union volunteers, however; it was to be used only in areas that had not produced their quota of volunteers. The law allowed a man to hire someone to serve in his place, or to purchase outright exemption for as little as $300. A phrase of the time, repeated by some critics of the volunteer Army in the 1970s, was "rich men's money and poor men's blood."

The draft was abandoned after the Civil War, and the Spanish-American War of 1898 was fought entirely with volunteers. In

---

[9] Lt. Col. Edward L. King (Ret.), *The Death of the Army* (1972), pp. 227-231.
[10] *The United States Army in Transition* (1973), p. 42.

1865, however, Brig. Gen. James Oakes, assistant provost marshal general for Illinois, had written an exhaustive report enumerating the mistakes of the Civil War draft and making recommendations for future mobilization. His report was not brought to light until more than 50 years later, when the manpower demands of World War I led to the Selective Service Act of 1917. It embodied many of his recommendations. About 75 per cent of the four million men who served in the newly expanded Army were conscripted under the Selective Service Act.

Planning for manpower procurement in the event of another emergency did not begin until nearly eight years after World War I. A joint Army and Navy Selective Service Committee in 1926 undertook to formulate and keep under constant review the proposal for a new selective service law and a plan for national and state selective service headquarters. When the Selective Training and Service Act was enacted on Sept. 16, 1940, more than a year before America's entry into World War II, a nationwide draft organization was ready for operation.

In a special message to Congress in March 1947, President Truman recommended that the 1940 draft act be allowed to expire. He made it plain that if voluntary enlistments did not provide adequate military strength, a return to conscription would be requested. Congress let the act lapse. But as the Cold War intensified, and voluntary enlistments failed to meet manpower needs, Truman went back to Congresss in March 1948 to ask reenactment of selective service legislation. After prolonged hearings and an all-night filibuster by Sen. Glen H. Taylor (D Idaho), who said the draft was "jeopardizing our future as a democratic free people," the Selective Service Act of 1948 became law. But few men were drafted until 1950, when hostilities broke out in Korea.[11]

After the onset of war in Korea, Secretary of Defense George C. Marshall asked Congress to lower the minimum draft age from 20 to 18 years and to extend the period of service from 21 to 27 months. Congress completed action on draft legislation within five months, and on June 19, 1951, President Truman approved the Universal Military Training and Service Act.

Unpopularity of Vietnam Call Ups; Nixon's Plan

The 1951 act extended the draft to July 1, 1955, and additional four-year extensions were approved by Congress with little opposition in 1955, 1959 and 1963. In 1964, President Johnson initiated a Pentagon study of alternatives to the draft, partially in response to Republican campaign promises to end it. The report was overtaken by events, however, and was never published.

---

[11] Draft calls were 20,348 in 1948 and 9,781 in 1949.

The military draft, due to expire July 1, 1967, became a subject of considerable controversy in 1966, when increasing numbers of draftees were becoming combat casualties in Vietnam.

Though criticism of the draft system became involved with protests against the Vietnam War, there was considerable opposition to the system itself. Some critics called for a broad overhaul of the system to correct inequities, while others contended that the draft should be abolished altogether and replaced by a highly paid, all-volunteer force.[12] Eleven days before the draft was due to expire, Congress on June 20, 1967, extended it for four more years, to July 1, 1971.

In his 1968 presidential campaign, Richard Nixon embraced the idea of a volunteer Army. It was brought to his attention by a young Republican economist, Martin Anderson, who opposed the draft on traditional conservative grounds that it constituted unwarranted interference by government in the lives of individuals. Donald Smith, writing in *Atlantic* magazine, described the political appeal of the idea:

> The more pragmatic wing of the Nixon team was pleased by the prospect of Nixon embracing a plan that would attract war-weary voters, and confuse and divide the antiwar movement....The proposal seemed sure to confound further an already splintered and dispirited Democratic Party. Liberals in Congress were split on the issue, some fearing that a volunteer force would encourage a President to use the Army recklessly...Some liberals sided with conservatives who opposed the draft as an invasion of civil liberties.... Some congressmen simply saw the volunteer force proposal as a painless way to cast an antiwar vote.[13]

Nixon endorsed the concept late in 1967 and issued a major policy declaration on the subject, written by Anderson, in a campaign speech in October 1968. Soon after his inauguration as President, Nixon appointed a commission headed by former Secretary of Defense Thomas S. Gates Jr. to investigate the feasibility of the all-volunteer proposal. The commission's report, in February 1970, confronted virtually every objection raised against an all-volunteer force, including the arguments that it would constitute a risk to national security and consist largely of poor blacks. The commission called the force feasible, financially sound and morally correct.

Last Draft Call and Law's Expiration in 1973

On the strength of the Gates Commission report, President Nixon began laying the groundwork for a volunteer Army, called VOLAR. The first step was to make military life more attractive

---

[12] See "Draft Law Revision," *E.R.R.*, 1966 Vol. I, pp. 440-461, and Congressional Quarterly's *Congress and the Nation*, Vol. II (1969), pp. 879-890.

[13] Donald Smith, "Reports and Comment: The Volunteer Army,"*Atlantic*, July 1974, p. 8.

Active Military Personnel

	June 30 1968	June 30, 1974	June 30, 1975 *	June 30, 1976 *
	(in thousands)			
Army	1,570	783	785	785
Navy	765	546	536	529
Marine Corps	307	189	196	196
Air Force	905	643	612	590
Total	3,547	2,161	2,129	2,100

* Estimated
SOURCE: Federal Budget, Fiscal Year 1976

with pay raises and enlistment bonuses, and by improving the quality of service life. The Gates Commission had suggested an end to induction authority by June 30, 1971, but the administration sought and Congress approved a two-year extension to July 1, 1973. The disengagement from Vietnam and an intensified recruitment campaign encouraged the administration to eliminate the draft six months ahead of schedule.

The last draft call went out in January 1973,[14] but the Army's recruiting results were unexpectedly dismal. In the first nine months of 1973 the Army consistently missed its recruiting goals, falling as low as 49 per cent in April, while the other services had no such trouble. Roger T. Kelley, director of Pentagon manpower policies in 1969-73, contended that the volunteer Army was being sabotaged from within. A variety of facts led others to be concerned as well: for example, the Army chose to move its recruiting command from Washington, D.C., to Chicago in June 1973, the first month of VOLAR and normally the best recruiting month of the year; officers in the recruiting command were not promoted or rewarded; recruiting shortfalls were carried over from one month to the next, thereby inflating the apparent size of successive monthly shortfalls; and the number of recruiters was reduced by almost 18 per cent in the first nine months after the draft ended. Kelley later commented:

> The draft system was more comfortable and secure, since all you had to do was reach into the well and call up more people whenever you had shortages. Military careerists could count on always having a sufficient number of people. The volunteer system puts you into competition with other employers and therefore it demands considerably more leadership than does the draft system.[15]

[14] The Army did not actually become an all-volunteer force until Nov. 22, 1974, when the last draftee was discharged.
[15] Quoted by Smith, *op. cit.*, pp. 7-8.

Army spokesmen discounted talk of sabotage, attributing their mistakes to inexperience. In October 1973, after the chairman of the Senate Armed Services Committee, John C. Stennis (D Miss.), had warned that the draft was not likely to be restored, Army Chief of Staff Gen. Creighton W. Abrams called a conference of major commanders and reportedly ordered them to push the volunteer system. The next month, the Army surpassed its recruiting goal by 4 per cent, and results since then do not seem to suggest that the Army will have difficulties meeting its quotas for the near future.

Prospects for the Volunteer Army

THE DECISION to put the Army once more on a volunteer basis has had a profound effect on service life. "During the decades of the draft," Secretary Callaway has said, "we gradually came to look upon a citizen's initial years of service as a period of sacrifice he owed to his country. That perception was reflected in the way the Army managed its people." Callaway told Congress this year he accepted the criticism that soldiers and their problems were mishandled. He pointed out that legislation, too, had reflected the attitude that service was supposed to be a sacrifice.

> Our first termers [Callaway continued] drew poverty wages; they had no allowances for family travel benefits; the government would not sponsor their dependents at overseas posts. All of this was done because it was generally felt that a draftee should serve an obligation, without regard to his own wishes or needs. This attitude may be acceptable during a war, but it is clearly an inappropriate policy for attracting volunteers to enlist for a longer time during a period of peace.[16]

Men and women entering the services were paid only about 60 per cent of what they would earn in civilian life. In effect, they were subsidizing the nation to the sum of about $2 billion annually. The Gates Commission report in 1970 recognized this inequity, and the Military Selective Service Act of 1971 provided incentive increases in military pay and allowances similar to those the commission had recommended. Recruit pay was increased about 60 per cent, and by fiscal 1972 it reached comparability with the average for 19-year-old civilian male workers. Base pay is now $344 monthly for recruits, and total military compensation may be 20 to 30 per cent higher because of allowances for dependents and housing, and such fringe benefits as free medical and dental care, a free retirement plan,

---

[16] Testimony before the House Committee on Armed Services, Feb. 26, 1975.

Examples of Military Compensation

Rank or Grade	Years of service	Dependents	Basic pay	Total compensation*
Officers				
General	26	1	$36,000	$43,544
Lieutenant general	26	2	36,000	43,487
Major general	26	2	36,000	43,487
Brigadier general	26	3	31,565	38,542
Colonel	26	3	27,727	33,743
Lieutenant colonel	20	3	21,856	27,009
Major	14	3	17,640	22,132
Captain	6	3	13,932	17,920
First lieutenant	2	2	9,580	12,984
Second lieutentant	less than 2	1	7,610	10,507
Enlisted personnel				
Sergeant major	22	3	13,666	17,815
Master sergeant	20	3	11,380	15,171
Sergeant, first class	18	3	9,907	13,412
Staff sergeant	14	3	8,428	11,752
Sergeant	4	2	6,156	9,348
Corporal	2	1	5,249	8,187
Private, first class	less than 2	0	4,781	7,020
Private, E-2	less than 2	0	4,601	6,703
Private, E-1	less than 2	0	4,129	6,156

* Includes quarters and subsistence allowances and tax advantages

SOURCE: Martin Binkin, Brookings Institutions study *The Military Pay Muddle.*

---

and discount-priced food and merchandise available in commissaries and post exchanges.

Other aspects of military life also have been changed. Some action has been taken to remedy such problems as lack of privacy, decaying barracks, unpalatable food, and "mickey mouse" duties such as KP—kitchen police—and weekend inspections. Uniforms are specially fitted, reveille formations have been abandoned, and beer and hamburgers are available at mess halls. Once a recruit has finished basic training, his Army experience is closer than ever before to that of an eight-hour-a-day, five-day-a-week job.

Such innovations have not been uniformly successful; an Army captain described his experience at Ft. Carson, Colo., in the early 1970s when experiments aimed at improving GI life were introduced: "Training had come to almost a complete halt. Some units were at 30 per cent strength, and they just put their equipment in storage. Field exercises were unheard of."[17] There is renewed emphasis on training, but the right combination of toughness and comfort has not yet been found at all posts; and some sergeants and officers fear that concern for civilian-style freedom and comfort will interfere with combat effectiveness.

[17] John Hotz, quoted in *The Wall Street Journal*, Jan. 15, 1975.

Education and job training have become increasingly important for attracting new recruits. Roger Kelley, before his retirement in 1973 as Assistant Secretary of Defense for Manpower and Reserve Affairs, told the House Armed Services Subcommittee on Recruiting and Retention that the two reasons most frequently given for enlisting were "to obtain a better opportunity for advanced educational training" and "to acquire a skill or trade valuable in civilian life." But the type of training offered by the Army, and the use to which such training is put, are potential sources of discontent and disillusionment.

According to a study cited by David B. Cortright in *The Progressive*, September 1973, some 13 per cent of the enlisted jobs have no civilian counterparts; overall, 80 per cent of the military jobs are in areas that account for only 11 per cent of all civilian jobs. The problem is made worse by the misuse of individual skills—the military's legendary propensity for putting square pegs in round holes.

In December 1973, a special Army office was established to examine these matters. It determined that in June 1972 there were 78,000 soldiers—16 per cent of the enlisted force—in jobs unsuited to their occupational specialties. This figure, according to Lt. Gen. Harold G. Moore, Deputy Chief of Staff for Personnel, was halved by December 1974. Such improvements are deemed vital not only because volunteer manpower is a limited and costly resource, but because inactivity or misuse of skill erodes the level of job satisfaction which must exist if soldiers are to remain in the Army.

Morale and Discipline in the Post-Vietnam Army

The change to a volunteer force has taken place at a time when the U.S. military is faced with profound problems that crystallized during the Vietnam period. Restiveness within the profession is combined with anti-military sentiments in society. For reasons in addition to its new all-volunteer makeup, the Army is at a crucial phase. "War does a great many things to the Army," the late Gen. Creighton W. Abrams told an interviewer in 1973. "It stretches it to its limits....a lack of know-how becomes widespread in the Army. Ethical and professional standards are diluted.... That's where the American Army is today: rebuilding its professional and ethical standards so that it's capable of doing its job."[18]

Some of the problems that surfaced in Vietnam still threaten the volunteer Army. Like American society in general, the armed forces were racked by outbreaks of racial violence in the late 1960s and early 1970s. Senior civilian and uniformed Pen-

---

[18] Interview with *U.S. News & World Report*, Aug. 6, 1973, p. 38.

Recruiting Ethics

"Selling a qualified young man on enlisting...is somewhat like the challenge of separating a person from his money." That phrase from the Marine Corps Recruiters' Handbook exposes a controversial aspect of the all-volunteer force. For in their efforts to sell the military life and meet their enlistment quotas, recruiters have been accused of misrepresenting the product.

"Many recruiters make alluring promises they have no authority to keep, or fail to mention the conditions that go along with various options and bonuses," David B. Cortright wrote in *The Progressive*, September 1973. And even the legitimate offers, like the Army's Project Ahead which enables recruits to get a college education mainly at the Army's expense, are pushed with massive advertising. The armed services spent $93 million in fiscal 1975 for advertising, more than General Motors did.

If young men and women are misled into enlisting, then the loser will be the military itself. Richard Stillman II wrote in *Public Administration Review*, May-June 1974, "In the near future perhaps the greatest source of minority frustration in the military will be spawned by the Pentagon's own recruitment efforts which tend to raise unwarranted expectations about the opportunities available in the armed services for minorities." With recruiting literature promising easy promotions, choice of job assignments, ample training opportunities and world travel, there are fears that the Pentagon may be "overselling" itself.

tagon officials have repeatedly stressed their commitment to racial equality, and several steps have been taken to deal with racial tension. A concerted effort has been made to encourage the opportunities for cultural diversity among minority groups and to promote faster communication of grievances. Moreover, the Pentagon has sought to increase the number of black senior officers. Perhaps most promising for the future, the Defense Race Relations Institute opened in May 1972 at Patrick Air Force Base to train 1,400 instructors annually in race relations.[19]

It is hoped that as the military becomes composed increasingly of mature, professional careerists, other disciplinary problems will also lessen. Results so far vary among units, but from July 1973 to the end of 1974 there was a decrease in nonjudicial punishments imposed throughout the Army, and AWOL[20] and desertion figures were halved, dropping them to the lowest level since 1969. In 1974 marijuana use and possession, the commonest drug offense, showed its first decline in three years.

---

[19] See Richard Stillman II, "Racial Unrest in the Military: The Challenge and the Response," *Public Administration Review*, May-June 1974.

[20] Absent Without Leave.

More subtle but no less serious problems of morale and discipline do not always show up in statistics. A number of journalists looking at the higher-paid volunteer Army have reported, as Donald Smith did in *Atlantic,* that "the almost unanimous opinion of the non-commissioned officers and commissioned officers at the company level whom I talked to (when out of range of senior officers) [was] that money has brought neither motivation nor discipline."

A former officer whose family name has long been associated with military command, Lucian K. Truscott IV, reported in *Harper's* magazine that, looking at Ft. Ord, Calif., he found "hope that there was really something afoot in the new volunteer Army." But at Ft. Carson, Colo., he quoted an enlisted man as expressing a common dismay: "Privates like us are telling sergeants and lieutenants where to get off. Nothing happens. They just take it.... There's just no discipline. It's all falling apart."[21]

These problems cannot be attributed solely to the quality of enlisted men, for new programs give misfits and malcontents the opportunity to leave the Army without stigma. Since the fall of 1973, Army programs have permitted enlisted men—both recruits and persons with up to 36 months of continuous service—to be separated with honorable or general discharges if they are unable to adjust to military life or meet its standards. But their officers must take the initiative.[22]

Many soldiers and civilians feel that ultimately it is the leaders of the volunteer army who must bear responsibility for failures in morale and discipline. "The war in Vietnam produced a generation of commanders weaned on the infamous 'body count,' and by 1970 lying in the Army had become standard operating procedure," wrote Truscott, who was then a lieutenant fresh out of West Point. In a volunteer Army, as in a conscripted one, it is the officers who must set the standards for such military virtues as pride in service, performance, and duty.

More Use of Civilians and Women in Military Jobs

Satisfactory recruiting statistics, assurances from the Pentagon, and the distraction of other, more pressing issues ensure that the all-volunteer Army will survive for the near future. However, if the return to a full-employment economy dries up the supply of enlistees, or if quality and morale suffer a dramatic decline, then pressures will build to bring back con-

---

[21] Lucian K. Truscott IV, "Notes On a Broken Promise," *Harper's,* July 1974, p. 22.

[22] An experimental program, Voluntary Release Option Test, gives enlistees the chance to request discharge (but not the right to discharge) after completing basic training. During the initial phases of the test, according to Lt. Gen. Moore, about 18 per cent elected discharge.

scription. This might take the form of a universal service system whereby a young person could choose between spending two years in the military or in a government-sponsored public service occupation. Any move to reinstate the draft, in whatever form, is likely to be politically unpopular, and it is likely that other options will be explored beforehand to alter the supply of recruits or the demand for them. Although physical standards could be relaxed if men were to be accepted for "limited duty" assignments, mental and moral qualifications could not be reduced so easily.

A more likely approach would be to decrease the demand for enlisted male personnel, and several steps have already been taken in this direction. One is to replace military men with civilians: in 1974 the Army completed the "civilianization" of 10,000 military jobs, and 4,000 others are now being converted. The role of women has also increased. Army plans for mid-1975 called for 41,000 women, over 5 per cent of the Army's authorized strength. In three years the number is expected to rise to 52,700, or 6.7 per cent.

The number of men reaching age 18 each year is expected to keep increasing until 1978. Then it will start to decline and reach a low point in 1986. This drop in available manpower has serious implications for recruiting. But an average annual increase of just 2,600 in the number of women recruited through the 1980s—equal to the average projected increase in the 1975-79 period—would reduce the required male enlistment ratio (volunteers to men available) in the late 1980s below the current ratio. With the expansion of the number of women in the Army has come an expansion of the number of occupations they can fill.

Only combat arms, or 36 of the 451 enlisted military occupational specialties, are closed to women. Even combat duties may in time be open to them. Both houses of Congress this year have approved amendments to a weapons procurement bill that would allow women to enter the U.S. Military, Naval and Air Force academies. Opponents argued that is a step toward putting women in combat, but to those who backed the amendment, the idea of women in service academies was an idea whose time had come.[23] Whether women are given combat responsibilities equal to men's will ultimately depend on social attitudes rather than military considerations. Similarly, the fate of the all-volunteer Army will depend largely on the attitudes of the citizenry from whom its soldiers will be drawn, and whom it is supposed to serve.

---

[23] See *Congressional Quarterly Weekly Report*, May 24, 1975, p. 1079.

Selected Bibliography

Books

Bradford, Zeb B. Jr., and Frederic J. Brown, *The United States Army In Transition*, Sage Publications, 1973.

Just, Ward, *Military Men*, Alfred A. Knopf, 1970.

King, Edward L., *The Death of the Army: A Pre-Mortem*, Saturday Review Press, 1972.

Articles

Cortright, David B., "The Military Recruitment Racket," *The Progressive*, September 1973.

"It's Sro at Army Recruiting Offices," *Business Week*, Feb. 24, 1975.

Klare, Michael T., "Can the Army Survive VOLAR?" *Commonweal*, Jan. 18, 1974.

McAuliffe, Kevin, "The Small Print of Enlistment," *The Nation*, May 4, 1974.

Sarkesian, Sam C., "Viet Nam and the Professional Military," *Orbis*, Spring 1974.

Smith, Donald, "Reports and Comment: The Volunteer Army," *Atlantic*, July 1974.

Stillman, Richard II, "Racial Unrest in the Military: The Challenge and the Response," *Public Administration Review*, May-June 1974.

"Suddenly—More Volunteers Than the Services Can Use," *U.S. News & World Report*, March 24, 1975.

Truscott, Lucian K. IV, "Notes On A Broken Promise," *Harper's*, July 1974.

Studies and Reports

"Accession Requirements and the Availability of Volunteers, 1975-1990," Office of the Assistant Secretary of Defense for Manpower and Reserve Affairs, Nov. 29, 1974.

"The Army 1974: Year-End Report," Department of the Army, 1975.

Binkin, Martin and John D. Johnston, "All-Volunteer Armed Forces: Progress, Problems and Prospects," Brookings Institution study for the U.S. Senate Committee on Armed Services, June 1, 1973.

Binkin, Martin, *The Military Pay Muddle*, Studies in Defense Policy, Brookings Institution, 1975.

Callaway, Howard H., Secretary of the Army, "The Posture of the Army," Statement before the U.S. House of Representatives Committee on Armed Services, Feb. 26, 1975.

Editorial Research Reports, "Draft Law Revision," 1966 Vol. I, p. 441; "Rebuilding the Army," 1971 Vol. II, p. 885.

Moore, Lt. Gen. Harold G., Deputy Chief of Staff for Personnel, Department of the Army, "Military Personnel," Statement before the U.S. Senate Appropriations Committee Subcommittee on Defense, March 13, 1975.

INDEX

A

185

INDEX

INDEX

INDEX

INDEX

U.S.-Soviet trade - 62
Vietnam and Nixon Doctrine - 58
Korea, South - 53, 57

L

Labor Supply. *See also* Bureau of
Labor Statistics (BLS); Education,
Vocational
  'Blue-collar blues' - 91
  'Brain drain' from poor nations -
  149-150
  'Dual labor market' - 91
  Education of industrial classes - 94
  Illegal aliens - 150-153
  Job banks - 102
  Manpower Development and
  Training Act (MDTA) of 1962 - 95
  Underemployment and entrapment
  feelings - 90
  Underemployment and recession - 87
  Underemployment as incurable
  problem - 100-102
  U.S. immigration policy - 148-149
Latin America
  Immigration patterns 1965-1973
  (table) - 148, 151
  Legal and illegal immigrants - 150-153
  Monroe Doctrine and - 55
  U.S. role as world's policeman - 56-57
League of Nations - 56
Lebanon. *See* Middle East
Legislative Branch. *See* Congress
Library of Congress
  Futures Division - 6
Lincoln, Abraham - 36-39

M

Mass transit. *See* Transporta-
tion
Massachusetts Tomorrow - 8
Media and Communications
  Electronic shopping - 83
  Forecasts of the past - 4
  New teaching techniques - 117-118
  Telecommunications revolution and
  rural migration - 10, 83
  Television and politics - 43
Medicine. *See also* Physicians
  Inequities of Medicaid - 130
  Medicare recipients (1975) - 129
  Origin of Medicaid - 137
  Problems of morals, medicine and
  health - 11
Middle East
  Emigration of Soviet Jews - 51
  Lebanon and U.S. global policy - 57,
  59
  Military sales - 48-49, 53[9]

Migration, Internal
  Collectivism - 70
  Declining farm population (1920-73)
  - 75
  Opening of the West - 74, 83, 154
  Rapidly growing nonmetropolitan
  regions (map) - 69
  Return migration to the South - 79
  Review of migration policy - 163
  Retirement communities - 72
  Urban growth restrictions - 10
  Urban-to-rural - 67-83
Military sales. *See* Foreign Affairs
Minorities
  Armed services recruitment ethics -
  181
  Bilingual education - 160
  Cultural pluralism - 162
  Ethnic militancy - 159
  Interest in basic education skills - 110-
  111
  Mexican-Americans - 152-153
  Nativist-immigrant issues - 155-158
  Survival of ethnic identity - 158-159
  Underemployment and job perform-
  ance - 91
  Virtues of ethnicity - 158, 162
Monroe Doctrine - 54-55
Morrill Act (1862) - 94
Moynihan, Daniel P. - 20, 61[25],
142[21], 159

N

National Alternative Schools Program
  - 107, 108-109-122
National Assessment of Educational
  Progress (NAEP) - 118
National Center for Urban Ethnic
  Affairs - 159
National Science Foundation (NSF)
  Controversy over MACOS - 123
  Immigrant physicians - 150
  Job outlook for college-educated - 90
  Long-range policy-making projections
  - 7, 8
Natural resources. *See* Environ-
ment
Nixon, Richard M.
  Detente and the Nixon Doctrine -
  58-59
  Greece involvement - 53
  Poll ratings (1962) - 37
  Presidential personality traits - 33-34
  Rural development - 77
  Social services - 138, 141
  Underemployment - 99
  Volunteer Army - 176
Nuclear Threat. *See also* Arms
Control
  Criticism of U.S. foreign policy - 48-49
  Energy problems - 13

INDEX

Kissinger policy on strategic weapons
- 50-51
Nuclear weapons sales - 62-63
Possibilities of world government - 20
World income redistribution - 4-5

O

Office of Technology Assessment (OTA)
- 6
Overseas Development Council - 19

P

Physicians. *See also* Medicine
Doctor-to-patient ratios - 150
Immigrant physicians - 150, 162
Oversupply of doctors - 90
'Vendor' payments to doctors - 137
Polls. *See also* Public Opinion Polls
Basic computation skills (17- to
35-year-olds) - 119
Britannica, future of capitalism - 16
Business' demand for college
graduates - 88
Cost of educating a student - 107
Future research methods - 7
Open schools survey (Long Island) -
114
Presidential greatness (Schlesinger
poll) - 37
Pollution - 5, 68
Population Policy. *See also* Migra-
tion, Internal
Commission on Population Growth
and the American Future - 78, 81-82
Immigration policy changes - 147, 148
'Limits to Growth' conferences - 14
Proposed immigration restrictions -
162-163
Trends in world growth rates - 5, 19
Trends in U.S. growth rates - 82
Zero Population Growth - 162
Post-industrial society. *See* Eco-
nomic Conditions
Presidency. *See* Executive Branch
Progressive Education Association -
116
**Project on the Predicament of Man-
kind** - 5
Public Opinion Polls. *See also* Polls
Allocation of resources, antitrust
issues - 23
Attitudes toward education - 108
Confidence in government - 14
Confidence in private enterprise
system - 16-17
Domestic v. foreign priorities - 59
Rise or decline of U.S. global power -
48

Rural-urban preferred residency - 78-
79
Truman popularity (1945) - 29
Voters' confidence in presidential
choices - 41
Public school system. *See* Education, Compulsory

R

Rand Corporation - 5, 7
Recessions. *See* War, Economic
Aspects
Religion
Disputes over textbooks, teaching
materials - 108
Ethnic enclaves - 155
Exodus from Old World - 154
Possibilities of world government - 20
Refugees
1948 Displaced Persons Act - 157
Emigration of Soviet Jews - 51
U.S. immigration policy - 148-149
Resources for the Future - 13
Rockefeller, John D. - 93, 163[26]
Rockefeller Foundation - 159
Roosevelt, Franklin D. *See also*
Great Depression
Poll ratings (1962) - 37
Presidential personality traits - 33-34,
39
Rural Affairs. *See also* Migration,
Internal
Economic development and farming
decline - 72-73, 74-75
Land conservation threat - 80
Recreation businesses and local
inflation - 80
Revitalization and development - 77
Urban-rural population division
(1790-1970) - 81

S

Schlesinger, James R. - 50, 53
Science and Technology. *See also*
Forecasting
Controversy over MACOS - 123
Employment outlook for college
graduates - 88-90
Philadelphia Centennial Exhibition
- 3
Problems of morals, medicine and
health - 11
Sputnik and National Defense
Education Act - 96, 118
Transition from urban to rural life -
71-72, 83
Seattle 2000 - 8
Selective Service System - 168, 175

INDEX

INDEX